Copyright and Publisher Information

Divine Conversations:
A Collection of 150 Prayers for Every Situation
Copyright © 2024
All rights reserved.

Unless otherwise indicated, all Scripture quotations are taken from the HOLY BIBLE, NEW INTERNATIONAL VERSION®. NIV®. Copyright© 1973, 1978, 1984 by International Bible Society. Used by permission of Zondervan. All rights reserved.

No part of this publication may be reproduced, interpreted, stored in a retrieval system, or transmitted, in any form or by any means, electronic, mechanical, photocopying or otherwise, without the prior written permission of the Author.

ISBN NO: 978-629-99692-0-4

Published by Norman J. Sinappen.
Email :normansinappen@gmail.com

Design and layout by E Concept Communications
www.e-concept.com.my

Printed in Slovakia.

AF091903

Dedication Page

To all prayer warriors around the world,

Your unwavering faith, fervent prayers, and relentless intercession inspire and uplift countless souls every day.

May your dedication to seeking God's will and standing in the gap for others be rewarded with abundant blessings and divine favor. Thank you for being beacons of light in a world in need of hope, and for demonstrating the transformative power of prayer.

This book is dedicated to you, with deep gratitude and heartfelt appreciation, for your invaluable contribution to God's kingdom.

May God continue to strengthen and guide you as you carry out your sacred calling.

Foreword by Rev. Dr. Steven Francis

I am proud and honored to have known Norman for many years as a God-fearing man who always desires to do the will of God. From his youth, he attempted many new endeavors to touch people for Jesus. His heart to reach out to others with the love of God around the nations is admirable.

I have seen and witnessed God's hand upon Norman in all that he has accomplished thus far. The Lord Jesus lifted him from a small city in Malaysia to where he is today, a testament to a man whose heart is after God's things.

Norman's dedication to God's work has elevated him as a leader through many entrepreneurial efforts and placed him in important leadership positions. I am amazed at how he makes time to go the extra mile to fulfill the burdens in his heart while working full-time in a world-class position and being a family man.
His dedication to excellence places him as a leader in kingdom business.

This book will tremendously help and encourage people in need of prayer. It is an excellent resource for parents to mentor their children in prayer. It is also a good resource for the Christian counselor who needs to pray and counsel clients or patients with the relevant scriptures. This book will also be a quick resource for busy executives who need to pray in all kinds of situations.

This book will be a powerful prayer resource for lay leaders in churches and home groups. It will give you the confidence to pray scriptural prayers that touch God's heart. I pray that God will use this book to inspire thousands to have the heart to pray. With such a resourceful book, you will have the courage to become a blessing to others with faith.

May God strengthen the Church with praying warriors.

Dr. Steven Francis,
D.Min, M. SocSc Counseling
Founder, Rivers of Life Apostolic Ministries, USA
Senior Pastor, Jesus My King Church, USA
Apostolic Lead, ROLAM Network, USA

Reader Reflections

I have had the privilege of knowing Norman for nearly a decade as his pastor here in Geneva, Switzerland. His deep passion for Jesus and the Scriptures inspires and encourages those around him, as well as his joy and laughter! His latest work, this book of prayers, is a testimony to his earnest desire to support fellow believers around the world in their prayer journeys.

Jesus constantly had to remind the disciples that the life of discipleship was one of dependence on God and this was manifested "only by prayer" (Mark 9:29). This collection is designed to aid believers in confronting life's diverse situations through prayer, enabling them to live a life anchored in prayerful dependence on God.

In an era that increasingly champions self-reliance, Norman's book serves as a vital reminder of the importance of being reliant on God. It provides believers with prayers suited for any circumstance, which can be personalized to meet the unique challenges we each face. Norman, thank you for blessing the church with this invaluable resource that will strengthen the faith of believers everywhere.

Pastor James Tetley
Crossroads Church, Geneva, Switzerland

Many believe the early Church engaged only in spontaneous prayer and worship, but this is not true. They also had written liturgies. Today, there is a need for systematic and organized prayer, as some people struggle to find the right words or appropriate scripture while praying. Norman's "Divine Conversations" serves as an excellent guide for organizing one's prayers for any occasion. I highly recommend this book to everyone who wish to draw closer to God through prayer.

Dr. S. A. Devasahayam, Ph.D.
Principal, Koinonia Leadership Training Institute, India

Reader Reflections

In Matthew 26:40, at Gethsemane, Jesus asked his disciples, "Could you not watch with Me in prayer for one hour?" However, the disciples fell asleep instead of praying. Their prayer lives transformed dramatically after receiving the Holy Spirit on Pentecost Day in the upper room. From then on, they prioritized prayer, which empowered them to complete their earthly mission successfully.

In today's world, if we want to live victoriously, we must also cultivate the discipline of prayer. Prayer is about conversing with Lord Jesus and expressing our heart's desires to Him. Despite our busy lives and competing priorities, Norman has written this prayer book with compassion to highlight the importance of prayer. Each prayer includes relevant scriptures that recall and claim God's promises.

I believe this prayer book will be a blessing to all who use it as a resource during their prayers. I commend Norman for setting this goal and completing the book despite his demanding full-time job at an international organization. I pray that the Holy Spirit's power will move mightily through this book and that the Lord will bless and anoint it. All glory to Lord Jesus, Amen.

Pas Selvadas Moses
Reheboth Bethel Church, Malaysia

Reader Reflections

I first met Norman some twenty years ago, a young man making his way into the world, determined to succeed, but also determined to seek and honour God. Now, twenty years later, I am privileged to pen these few paragraphs for this book. It is a collection of prayers for different situations, prayers that spring forth from Norman's rich experiences with God and His Word in the crucible of this journey that we call 'life.'

Our prayers are the expressions of our highest hopes in life. They are expressions of our deepest concerns and fears amidst the intricacies, challenges and heartbreaks of life. They also reveal our understandings of who God is - who we perceive Him to be and how we understand Him to act.

However, more than that, our prayers should be effectual. More than the mere release of our inner aspirations or of our ideas about God, our prayers are meant to draw us into a deeper fellowship with the Almighty. They are also meant to elicit His intervention into our human affairs. For this to happen, our prayers must align with God's will and God's ways.

On this basis, I commend this collection of prayers thoughtfully crafted by Norman. These are prayers shaped by his personal journey with God, as he navigated through the ups and downs of life where he has found God's faithfulness and interventions to be more than abundant. These are prayers shaped by his reflections on different passages of God's Word, passages that he effectively weaves into the different prayers for different situations.

Rev. Chan Nam Chen (PhD)
Executive Director, AsiaCMS

Reader Reflections

Welcome, you all Prayer Warriors, to this sacred collection of prayers. Within these pages, you will discover a treasury of words from the Bible that can comfort and bring solace to the prayer warriors. No matter, whether you seek solace in times of uncertainty, gratitude in moments of abundance, or guidance on your spiritual journey, this prayer book offers a sanctuary of words to uplift your heart and soul.

Prayer is an universal language that transcends boundaries, inviting us to pause, reflect, and commune with the divine. In our busy lives, these moments of quiet contemplation can be transformative, offering clarity, peace, and a renewed sense of purpose. Each prayer contained herein has been carefully selected to resonate with the deepest aspirations of the human spirit.

As Jesus gives everyone a call to come to Him in the Gospel by Mathew 11:28-30, let us carry these points of prayers that He shall address and equip us with the Grace which is sufficient, His Strength replacing all the weaknesses.

As you journey through these pages, may you find resonance with the prayers that speak to your soul. May they serve as companions on your path, offering strength in times of adversity and celebration in times of joy. Let this book be not just a collection of words, but a cherished companion on your spiritual quest, guiding you toward a deeper connection with the sacred.

May these prayers inspire you to cultivate compassion, foster gratitude, and embody love in all aspects of your life. May they remind you of the beauty of the human spirit and the infinite possibilities that unfold when we open our hearts in prayer.

With heartfelt blessings,
Dr. K.Martina Rani
Professor,
School of Management
Karunya University, Coimbatore.

Preface

Welcome to **"Divine Conversations: A Collection of 150 Prayers for Every Situation."** In the hustle and bustle of life, prayer serves as a lifeline—a direct connection to our Creator, the One who hears our every word and knows the depths of our hearts. Prayer is not just a religious ritual; it's a heartfelt dialogue with the Almighty, a source of comfort, guidance, and strength in every season of life.

This book is a labor of love—a compilation of prayers carefully crafted to address a variety of topics and issues that we encounter on our journey through life. Whether you're facing challenges, celebrating victories, seeking guidance, or simply yearning for a deeper connection with God, you'll find prayers here to resonate with your heart and lift your spirit.

Each prayer is a reflection of the human experience—raw, honest, and vulnerable. They speak to the joys and sorrows, the hopes and fears that we all encounter along life's winding path. From prayers for healing and provision to prayers for wisdom and peace, this book covers a wide array of topics to meet you right where you are.

But more than just words on a page, these prayers are an invitation—to draw near to the One who holds the universe in His hands, to pour out your heart before Him, and to experience His presence in a profound and transformative way. As you journey through these pages, may you be inspired to cultivate a deeper, more intimate relationship with God—one that sustains you through every trial and rejoices with you in every triumph.

As the psalmist wrote in Psalm 145:18, "The Lord is near to all who call on him, to all who call on him in truth." May this truth resonate in your heart as you engage in divine conversation through prayer.

So, dear reader, I invite you to embark on this sacred journey of prayer - to open your heart, lift your voice, and experience the power of divine conversation. May these prayers be a guiding light on your path, leading you ever closer to the heart of God.

Remember, Jesus loves you, and I love you too!
Norman J. Sinappen

Acknowledgement

First and foremost, I would like to express my deepest gratitude to God, the source of all inspiration, wisdom, and creativity. Without His guidance and grace, this book would not have been possible.

I am immensely thankful for my family and friends who have supported and encouraged me throughout this journey. Your unwavering love and belief in me have been a constant source of strength and motivation.

I extend heartfelt appreciation to the pastors, mentors, and spiritual guides who have poured into my life, imparting wisdom and knowledge that has enriched my understanding of prayer and deepened my relationship with God.

A special thank you to the readers whose feedback and encouragement have shaped the content of this book. Your insights and perspectives have been invaluable in refining the prayers and ensuring their relevance to a wide audience.

Special thanks to Rev. Dr. Steven Francis for being a strong inspiration and for always being present providing continuous encouragement, support and guidance.

Special thanks to Mr. Tharmaraj Rajandran. Thank you for kicking off this project with your blessing prayer.

I would like to extend my heartfelt gratitude to my uncle, Mr. Daniel Vanathiah, for his invaluable proofreading assistance. Your support has been immensely appreciated. Thank you!

Lastly, I acknowledge the countless individuals whose prayers and intercession have paved the way for the manifestation of God's purposes in my life and in the lives of others. Your faithfulness in prayer has made an eternal impact, and I am deeply grateful for your partnership in the ministry of prayer.

May God bless each of you abundantly and continue to use this book as a tool to draw hearts closer to Him and ignite a passion for prayer in every reader.

Thank you!

Table Of Contents

Dedication Page	2
Foreword by Rev. Dr. Steven Francis	3
Readers' Reflections	4
Preface	8
Acknowledgement	9
Table of Contents	10
Addiction	15
Baby Dedication	16
Baby Naming Ceremony	17
Baby Shower	18
Before Bed or Sleep	19
Before Driving	20
Belief	21
Birthday	22
Business	23
Church Leaders	24
Church	25
Clarity and Understanding	26
Closing Prayer	27
Communication	28
Compassion	29
Confession	30
Contentment	31
Dream Big: Setting High Goals	32
Daily Bread	33
Daughter	34
Dedication to Ministry	35
Depression	36
Discipline	37
Disruptions	38
Earth and Universe	39
Emergencies	40
End of Abortion	41
End of Violence and War	42
Enemies	43
Engagement Couples	44
Events or Parties	45
Exams	46
Facing Difficult Decisions	47
Faith	48
Family	49
Fasting	50
Father	51
Fear	52
Financial Interventions	53
Forgiveness	54
Freedom	55
Friends	56
Funeral or Deceased	57
Future Spouse	58

Table Of Contents

Future Plans	59
Generosity	60
Gentleness	61
Gift of Speech	62
God's Love	63
God's Will be done on Earth	64
Good Weather	66
Government and Politicians	67
Grace	68
Grandma (Grandmother)	69
Grandpa (Grandfather)	70
Gratitude	71
Grievances	72
Growth	73
Happiness	74
Healing	75
Health	76
Heart for Missions	77
Heaven	78
Holy Communion	79
Holy Spirit	80
Home	82
Homeless	84
Honesty and Integrity	86
Hope and Courage	87
Human Trafficking	88
Humility or Staying Humble	90
Hunger	91
Husband	92
Ideas	93
Inspiration	94
Jealousy	95
Job Interview	96
Journey Mercy	97
Justice	98
Kindness	99
Leadership Skills	100
Learning the Word of God	101
Loneliness	102
Love	103
Lust	104
Marriage or Wedding	106
Managers and Supervisors	107
Mercy	108
Ministry	109
Miracle	110
Missionaries	111
Morning - new day	113
Mother	114
Neighbour	115

Table Of Contents

Obedience	116
Opening Prayer	117
Opportunities	118
Passion and Purpose	119
Pastor	120
Patience	121
Peace	122
Perseverance	123
Poverty	124
Power	126
Praising God	127
Pray for the Lost	128
Prisoners	129
Prosperity	130
Protection over Marriage	131
Purity	132
Racism	133
Rebuking curses in our lives	134
Rebuking evil spirits	136
Receiving Prophetic Words and Revelations	137
Rejection	138
Relatives	139
Renewal of Mind	140
Responsibility	141
Restoration	142
Revival	143
Salvation for the Unsaved	145
Saying Grace before a meal	146
School and Education	147
Self-Control	148
Self-Respect and Self Esteem	149
Servant's Heart	150
Siblings	151
Sick	152
Signs and Wonders	153
Son	154
Spiritual Awareness	155
Spiritual Gifts	156
Spiritual Warfare	157
Strength to Forgive Others	158
Strength	159
Submission	160
Success	161
Teachers	162
Temptations	163
Thanksgiving	164
The Persecuted	165
Unity	166
Victims of Disaster	167
Victory	168

Table Of Contents

Wife	169
Wildlife and Animals	170
Wisdom	171
Workplace	172
Worship Choir and Music Team	174
World Peace	175
Thank You	176
About The Author	177

Prayer for
Baby Dedication

Heavenly Father,

We come before You today with our hearts full of gratitude for the precious gift of this child, **[Child's Name]**, whom we dedicate to You this day. Thank You for entrusting **[Child's Name]** into the loving care of **[Parent's Names]**, who have committed themselves to raising **[him/her]** in the ways of Your love and truth.

Lord, we dedicate **[Child's Name]** to You, acknowledging that **[he/she]** is a gift from You and belongs ultimately to You. We pray for Your guidance and wisdom for **[Parent's Names]** as they nurture and teach **[him/her]** in Your ways. May they be filled with Your love, patience, and grace as they seek to raise **[Child's Name]** in a home that honors You.

We pray for **[Child's Name]**'s future, that **[he/she]** would grow in wisdom and stature, and in favor with You and with others. May **[he/she]** come to know You personally at an early age and walk in Your ways all the days of **[his/her]** life.

As it is written in **Proverbs 22:6, "Start children off on the way they should go, and even when they are old, they will not turn from it."** Lord, we also pray for **[Child's Name]**'s extended family and friends who are gathered here today.

May they be faithful witnesses and sources of support and encouragement for **[Parent's Names]** as they raise **[him/her]**. We dedicate this child to You, Lord, trusting in Your promise to watch over **[him/her]** and to be **[his/her]** ever-present help in times of need.

May **[Child's Name]** grow to be a blessing to others and a shining light in this world, reflecting Your love and grace to all **[he/she]** encounters.

In Jesus' name we pray,
Amen.

Prayer for
Addiction

Heavenly Father,

I come before You humbled by Your grace and glory, acknowledging my struggle with addiction and recognizing my need for Your intervention and healing. Your Word teaches us that You are our refuge and strength, an ever-present help in times of trouble as mentioned in **Psalm 46:1**. Today, I seek refuge in You, asking for Your strength to overcome this addiction that has gripped my life.

Lord, You have promised us in **1 John 1:9** that if we confess our sins, You are faithful to forgive us and to cleanse us from all unrighteousness. I confess my addiction to You, knowing that You are merciful and compassionate, ready to extend Your grace to those who come to You in repentance.

Father, I pray for the strength to resist the temptation of addiction. Your Word assures us in **1 Corinthians 10:13** that no temptation has overtaken us except what is common to mankind, and You are faithful; You will not let us be tempted beyond what we can bear. But when we are tempted, You will also provide a way out so that we can endure it. Strengthen me, Lord, to walk away from the pull of addiction and to choose the path of righteousness.

Lord, I surrender my will and my desires to You, asking for Your Holy Spirit to fill me with the power to overcome this addiction. Your Word teaches us that we are more than conquerors through Christ who loves us **(Romans 8:37)**. May I experience the victory that comes from trusting in You and relying on Your strength.

Father, I pray for Your healing touch to break the chains of addiction that bind me. Your Word in **Isaiah 53:5** declares that by Jesus' wounds, we are healed. I claim this promise over my life, believing that You have the power to set me free from the bondage of addiction.

Lord, I commit my journey to recovery into Your hands, trusting in Your faithfulness to walk with me every step of the way. Help me to lean on You, to seek Your guidance, and to find strength in Your Word as I strive for freedom from addiction.

In Jesus' name, I pray,
Amen.

Prayer for
Baby Shower

Heavenly Father,

We gather before You today with our hearts full of joy and anticipation as we celebrate the arrival of the baby, a precious gift from Your loving hands. Thank You, Lord, for the miracle of new life and for the blessing of this little one who will soon join our lives.

Lord, we lift up *[Parent's Names]*, the soon-to-be parents, as they prepare to welcome their child into the world. Grant them wisdom, patience, and strength as they embark on this journey of parenthood. Surround them with Your love and peace, guiding them in every decision they make. As it is written in **James 1:5, "If any of you lacks wisdom, you should ask God, who gives generously to all without finding fault, and it will be given to you."**

We also pray for the baby, who is fearfully and wonderfully made in Your image. May the child grow strong and healthy in the womb and may the child's arrival bring joy and blessings to all.

As it is written in **Psalm 139:13-14, "For you created my inmost being; You knit me together in my mother's womb. I praise you because I am fearfully and wonderfully made; Your works are wonderful, I know that full well."** Lord, we ask for Your provision and protection over *[Parent's Names]* and their baby, in the days ahead. Help them to lean on You for support and to trust in Your perfect plan for their lives.

As it is written in **Philippians 4:19, "And my God will meet all your needs according to the riches of his glory in Christ Jesus."** As we gather together to shower *[Parent's Names]* with blessings, gifts and love, may this be a time of joyous celebration and sweet fellowship. May our words and actions reflect Your love and grace, encouraging and uplifting them as they prepare for the arrival of their little one.

We commit them into Your loving care, trusting in Your faithfulness to watch over them and to guide them in the days ahead.

In Jesus' name we pray,
Amen.

Prayer for Baby Naming Ceremony

Heavenly Father,

We gather before You today with our hearts overflowing with gratitude and joy as we celebrate the gift of new life and the blessing of this naming ceremony. Your Word in **Psalm 127:3** reminds us, **"Children are a heritage from the Lord, offspring a reward from him."** We thank You for the precious child, *[Child's Name]*, whom You have entrusted into our care.

Lord, we dedicate *[Child's Name]* to You, acknowledging that *he/she* is a gift from You and belongs ultimately to You. Your Word in **Proverbs 22:6** instructs us, **"Start children off on the way they should go, and even when they are old they will not turn from it."**

We pray for Your guidance and wisdom for the parents, *[Parents' Names]*, as they nurture and teach *[Child's Name]* in Your ways.

Father, we ask for Your blessings upon *[Child's Name]*'s future. May *he/she* grow in wisdom and stature, and in favor with You and with others, as Your Word mentions about Jesus in **Luke 2:52**. May *[Child's Name]* come to know You personally at an early age and walk in Your ways all the days of *his/her* life.

Lord, we also lift up *[Child's Name]*'s extended family and friends who are gathered here today. May they be faithful witnesses and sources of support and encouragement for *[Parents' Names]* as they raise **[Child's Name]**.

We dedicate this child to You, Lord, trusting in Your promise to watch over him/her and to be *his/her* ever-present help in times of need.

May *[Child's Name]* grow to be a blessing to others and a shining light in this world, reflecting Your love and grace to all *he/she* encounters.

In Jesus' name we pray,
Amen.

Prayer for
Before Driving

Heavenly Father,

As I prepare to embark on this journey, I come before You with a heart filled with gratitude for the gift of mobility and the privilege of travel. Your word teaches us in **Proverbs 3:5-6, "Trust in the Lord with all your heart and lean not on your own understanding; in all your ways submit to him, and he will make your paths straight."**

I commit myself and my journey into Your hands, trusting in Your guidance and protection.

Lord, I ask for Your presence to accompany me as I drive. Grant me wisdom and discernment to make safe and responsible decisions on the road. Help me to be attentive and focused, free from distractions that may hinder my ability to drive safely.

Father, I pray for protection over my vehicle and all who travel with me. Surround us with Your angels, guarding us from accidents, hazards, and unforeseen dangers.

Your word assures us in **Psalm 91:11-12, "For he will command his angels concerning you to guard you in all your ways; they will lift you up in their hands, so that you will not strike your foot against a stone."**

May I be a responsible and courteous driver, showing kindness and patience to others on the road. Help me to obey traffic laws and to drive with respect for the safety and well-being of all. Guide my hands and feet as I navigate the roads, keeping me alert and prepared for any challenges that may arise.

Lord, I thank You for Your promise to never leave nor forsake us **(Hebrews 13:5)**. As I journey, may I sense Your presence with me, bringing peace to my heart and assurance to my soul.

Help me to trust in Your providence and to surrender all my cares and concerns into Your loving hands.

In Jesus' name, I pray,

Amen.

Prayer for
Before Bed or Sleep

Heavenly Father,

As I prepare to rest my head and surrender to sleep, I come before You in humble gratitude for this day You have graciously given me. Your word reminds us in **Psalm 4:8, "In peace I will lie down and sleep, for you alone, Lord, make me dwell in safety."** I trust in Your loving care and protection as I enter into this time of rest.

As I reflect on the events of today, Lord, I thank You for the blessings and challenges of this day. I acknowledge Your presence in every moment, guiding me, sustaining me, and granting me strength. I recognize Your faithfulness and goodness in all things.

Father, I confess any sins or shortcomings of this day and ask for Your forgiveness and cleansing. Your word assures us in **1 John 1:9, "If we confess our sins, he is faithful and just and will forgive us our sins and purify us from all unrighteousness."** Wash me clean with Your mercy and grace and help me to walk in righteousness each day.

Lord, I commit my worries, fears, and anxieties into Your hands. Your word instructs us in **Philippians 4:6-7, "Do not be anxious about anything, but in every situation, by prayer and petition, with thanksgiving, present your requests to God. And the peace of God, which transcends all understanding, will guard your hearts and your minds in Christ Jesus."** Grant me Your peace that surpasses all understanding, guarding my heart and mind in Christ Jesus.

As I lay down to sleep, I surrender my cares and concerns to You, knowing that You are my refuge and strength. May Your presence surround me, protecting me from all harm and evil. Your word promises in **Psalm 91:11-12, "For he will command his angels concerning you to guard you in all your ways; they will lift you up in their hands, so that you will not strike your foot against a stone."**

Lord, I trust in Your provision for tomorrow, knowing that Your mercies are new every morning **(Lamentations 3:22-23)**. May I awake refreshed and renewed, ready to serve You with joy and obedience.

In Jesus' name, I pray,
Amen.

Prayer for Birthday

Heavenly Father,

I come before You today with heart full of gratitude and joy as we celebrate the precious gift of life that You have bestowed upon *[Name]*. Thank You for the years of blessings, experiences, and growth that You have granted *him/her*.

Lord, as *[Name]* marks another year of life, I ask for Your continued guidance, protection, and provision in *his/her* journey ahead. May Your loving presence surround *him/her* every step of the way, filling *his/her* heart with peace and *his/her* soul with joy.

I pray, O Lord, that You would grant *[Name]* wisdom, discernment, and strength for the challenges he/she may face in the coming year. Help him/her to walk in the path of righteousness and to fulfill the purpose and plans You have ordained for *his/her* life.

Lord, Your Word reminds us in **Psalm 20:4, "May he give you the desire of your heart and make all your plans succeed."** I ask that You fulfill the desires of *[Name]*'s heart according to Your will and bless *him/her* abundantly in every aspect of *his/her* life.

May this birthday be a reminder of Your unfailing love and faithfulness and may *[Name]* continue to grow in grace and wisdom with each passing year. Surround *him/her* with Your peace, fill *him/her* with Your joy, and bless *him/her* with every good thing from above.

In Jesus' name, I pray.
Amen.

Prayer for Belief

Heavenly Father,

We come before You with hearts full of gratitude for the gift of faith and belief that You have given us. Your word tells us in **Ephesians 2:8-9** that it is by grace we have been saved through faith, and this is not our own doing; it is the gift of God, not a result of works, so that no one may boast.

Lord, we thank You for the faith that You have planted within us, and we pray that You would strengthen and deepen our belief in You and Your promises. Help us to trust You more fully, knowing that You are faithful and true to Your word. Father, we pray for a belief that moves mountains, as Jesus taught us in **Matthew 17:20**. May our faith be strong and unwavering, trusting in Your power to overcome any obstacle or challenge that we may face. Lord, we pray for a belief that perseveres through trials and tribulations, as **James 1:3-4** tells us that the testing of our faith produces steadfastness, and that steadfastness must have its full effect, so that we may be perfect and complete, lacking in nothing. Help us to endure with patience and perseverance, knowing that You are with us in every trial and will never leave us nor forsake us.

Father, we pray for a belief that leads to obedience, as Your word tells us in **Hebrews 11:8** that by faith Abraham obeyed when he was called to go out to a place that he was to receive as an inheritance. May our faith be demonstrated by our obedience to Your word and Your will in every area of our lives. Lord, we pray for a belief that bears fruit, as Jesus taught us in **John 15:5** that whoever abides in Him and He in them bears much fruit, for apart from Him we can do nothing. May our lives be characterized by love, joy, peace, patience, kindness, goodness, faithfulness, gentleness, and self-control, bearing witness to the transforming power of Your Spirit within us. Father, we pray for a belief that leads to eternal life, as Your word assures us in **John 3:16** that whoever believes in Your Son, Jesus Christ, shall not perish but have eternal life. May we hold to this promise with unwavering faith, knowing that You are faithful to fulfill all that You have promised. Lord, we thank You for the gift of belief and for the assurance of salvation that it brings. May our faith continue to grow and deepen as we walk with You each day, trusting in Your goodness and Your love.

In Jesus' name, we pray,
Amen.

Prayer for Church Leaders

Heavenly Father,

We come before You with hearts full of gratitude for the leaders You have appointed to shepherd and guide our church family. Your word reminds us in **Hebrews 13:17, "Obey your leaders and submit to them, for they are keeping watch over your souls, as those who will have to give an account. Let them do this with joy and not with groaning, for that would be of no advantage to you."**

Lord, we lift up our church leaders to You, knowing that they carry a heavy burden of responsibility. Grant them wisdom, discernment, and understanding as they seek to lead and serve according to Your will. Help them to remain steadfast in their faith and reliant on Your Spirit for guidance.

Father, we pray for their spiritual well-being. Strengthen their relationship with You, Lord, and fill them afresh with Your Holy Spirit each day. Protect them from spiritual attacks and give them discernment to recognize and resist the plans of the enemy.

We ask for unity among our church leaders, Lord, that they may be of one mind and one accord as they seek to fulfill the mission and vision of our church.

May their interactions be marked by love, humility, and mutual respect, reflecting the unity of the body of Christ.

Lord, we pray for their families as well. May they experience Your peace, provision, and protection in abundance. Strengthen the bonds of love within their families and grant them grace to navigate the challenges of ministry life.

Father, we thank You for the sacrificial service of our church leaders. May they be encouraged and uplifted by the support and prayers of the congregation.

Help us to honor and respect them, Lord, as they faithfully fulfill the calling You have placed on their lives.

In Jesus' name, we pray,
Amen.

Prayer for Business

Heavenly Father,

We come before You today with hearts full of gratitude for the opportunities and resources You have blessed us with, including the work and business ventures entrusted to us. We recognize that every good gift comes from You, and we acknowledge that without You, we can do nothing.

As it is written in **James 1:17, "Every good and perfect gift is from above, coming down from the Father of the heavenly lights, who does not change like shifting shadows."** Lord, we lift up *[Name]*, and his business into Your hands. We pray for Your wisdom, guidance, and favor to be upon him in all his endeavors. Grant him the wisdom to make wise decisions, integrity to conduct his affairs with honesty and transparency, and diligence to lead and utilize his resources well.

As it is written in **Proverbs 3:5-6, "Trust in the Lord with all your heart and lean not on your own understanding; in all your ways submit to him, and he will make your paths straight."** Father, we ask for Your blessing upon *[Name]*'s business. May it be a place where Your principles of love, justice, and compassion are upheld. Bless the work of his hands and the efforts of his employees, that they may prosper and be a blessing to others.

As it is written in **Proverbs 16:3, "Commit to the Lord whatever you do, and he will establish your plans."** Guard *[Name]* against the temptations and pressures of the business world. Protect him from greed, selfish ambition, and dishonest practices. May his business be a beacon of light in a world that often prioritizes profit over people. As it is written in **Proverbs 11:3, "The integrity of the upright guides them, but the unfaithful are destroyed by their duplicity."**

Lord, we also pray for *[Name]*'s customers, suppliers, and all those who come into contact with or engaged with his business. May they experience Your love, mercy, and goodness through their interactions with him. As it is written in **Psalm 145:9, "The Lord is good to all; he has compassion on all he has made."** Above all, help [Name] to seek first Your kingdom and Your righteousness, trusting that as he does, all these things will be added unto him. As mentioned in **Matthew 6:33, "But seek first the kingdom of God and his righteousness, and all these things will be added to you."**

May his life and his business bring glory to Your name and further the work of Your kingdom on earth. We commit *[Name]* and his business into Your hands, trusting in Your faithfulness to guide, protect, and prosper him according to Your will.

In Jesus' name we pray,
Amen.

Prayer for
Clarity and Understanding

Heavenly Father,

We come before You with humble hearts, seeking Your divine understanding and wisdom. Your Word reminds us in **Proverbs 2:6, "For the Lord gives wisdom; from his mouth come knowledge and understanding."** We acknowledge that true understanding comes from You alone, and we seek Your guidance in all aspects of our lives.

Lord, as mentioned in **Psalm 119:105** Your Word is a lamp to our feet and a light to our path. Grant us understanding as we delve into Your Word, that we may discern Your truths and apply them to our lives. Help us to meditate on Your Word, day and night, as **Psalm 119:130** declares, **"The unfolding of your words gives light; it gives understanding to the simple."**

Father, in moments of confusion and uncertainty, we ask for Your clarity and insight. **Proverbs 3:5-6** reminds us to trust in You with all our hearts and not to lean on our own understanding, but to acknowledge You in all our ways, and You will direct our paths. Grant us the discernment to recognize Your leading and the courage to follow where You guide us.

Lord Jesus, You promised us in **John 14:26** to send the Holy Spirit, the Advocate, to teach us all things and to remind us of everything You have said. We invite the Holy Spirit to dwell within us, illuminating Your truth and deepening our understanding of Your teachings for our lives.

Help us, O Lord, to seek understanding not only for our own benefit but also to share Your wisdom with others. As it says in **Proverbs 11:30, "The fruit of the righteous is a tree of life, and the one who is wise saves lives."** May we be vessels of Your understanding and grace, bringing hope and healing to those around us.

Finally, Father, we pray for humility as we seek understanding, recognizing that Your ways are higher than our ways and Your thoughts higher than our thoughts as mentioned in **Isaiah 55:8-9**. May Your wisdom guide us in all our endeavors, that we may bring glory to Your name.

In Jesus' name, we pray,
Amen.

Prayer for
Church

Heavenly Father,

We come before You today with hearts full of gratitude for the gift of our church family. Thank You for bringing us together as a community of believers, united in love and faith. As it is written in **Hebrews 10:24-25, "And let us consider how we may spur one another on toward love and good deeds, not giving up meeting together, as some are in the habit of doing, but encouraging one another—and all the more as you see the day approaching."** Lord, we pray for our church. May it be a place where Your presence is felt and Your name is glorified. Fill our sanctuary with Your Spirit, and may every worship service, fellowship gathering, and ministry opportunity be marked by Your grace and truth. As it is written in **Psalm 26:8, "Lord, I love the house where you live, the place where your glory dwells."** Father, we pray for our pastors, leaders, and volunteers. Grant them wisdom, discernment, and strength as they serve and shepherd Your flock. May they be led by Your Spirit and guided by Your word in all that they do. As it is written in **1 Peter 5:2-3, "Be shepherds of God's flock that is under your care, watching over them—not because you must, but because you are willing, as God wants you to be; not pursuing dishonest gain, but eager to serve; not lording it over those entrusted to you, but being examples to the flock."**

Lord, we lift up our congregation to You. Bind us together in unity and love, and help us to support and encourage one another in our faith journeys. May we be known by our love for one another and our commitment to following Jesus. As it is written in **John 13:34-35, "A new command I give you: Love one another. As I have loved you, so you must love one another. By this everyone will know that you are my disciples, if you love one another."** Father, we pray for those in our community who do not yet know You. May our church be a beacon of light in the darkness, shining Your love and truth to all who are lost and searching. Use us as instruments of Your grace and mercy, reaching out to those in need and sharing the hope found in Jesus Christ.

As it is written in **Matthew 5:14-16, "You are the light of the world. A town built on a hill cannot be hidden. Neither do people light a lamp and put it under a bowl. Instead they put it on its stand, and it gives light to everyone in the house. In the same way, let your light shine before others, that they may see your good deeds and glorify your Father in heaven."** Lord, we ask for Your protection and provision over our church. Guard us against the attacks of the enemy and provide for our every need according to Your riches in glory. As it is written in **Philippians 4:19, "And my God will meet all your needs according to the riches of his glory in Christ Jesus."**

We commit our church into Your hands, trusting in Your faithfulness to guide, protect, and empower us to fulfill Your purposes in our community and beyond.

In Jesus' name we pray,
Amen.

Prayer for Communication

Heavenly Father,

I come before You today, recognizing the importance of communication in our relationships and in our walk with You. Your Word teaches us the power of our words and the significance of how we communicate with one another.

Lord, I pray that You would guide my words and my thoughts as I communicate with others. Help me to speak with grace and kindness, just as You have shown us in Your Son, Jesus Christ. We read in **Colossians 4:6 "Let your conversation be always full of grace, seasoned with salt, so that you may know how to answer everyone."** Teach me to use my words to build others up, rather than tearing them down as reminded in **Ephesians 4:29**.

Father, Your Word in **James 1:19**, instructs us to be quick to listen and slow to speak. Give me the patience to truly listen to others, to hear their hearts, and to understand their perspectives. Help me to communicate with empathy and compassion, seeking to understand before seeking to be understood. Lord, I pray for wisdom in my communication, knowing that the tongue has the power to bring life or death as mentioned in **Proverbs 18:21**. May my words be filled with wisdom and discernment, reflecting Your truth and love in every conversation.

Father, I ask for humility in my communication, recognizing that I am not always right and that I have much to learn from others. **Philippians 2:3** says **"Do nothing out of selfish ambition or vain conceit. Rather, in humility value others above yourselves"**. Help me to admit when I am wrong, to ask for forgiveness when needed, and to extend grace to those who may offend me.

Lord, I pray for unity in our communication as believers, that we may speak with one voice and one heart, proclaiming Your truth and sharing Your love with the world as stated in **1 Corinthians 1:10**. Help us to communicate in a way that brings glory to Your name and draws others into a strong relationship with You. Thank You, Father, for the gift of communication and for the opportunity to speak and listen to one another. May our words always be pleasing to You and edifying to those around us.

In Jesus' name, I pray,
Amen.

Prayer for
Closing Prayer

Heavenly Father,

As we prepare to depart from this place, we thank You for the time we've shared together in prayer. We are grateful for Your presence among us and for the ways You have spoken to our hearts.

As it is written in **Matthew 18:20, "For where two or three gather in my name, there am I with them."**

As we go our separate ways, may Your love go with us. Help us to carry the spirit of this gathering into our daily lives, shining Your light wherever we go. As it is written in **Matthew 5:16, "In the same way, let your light shine before others, that they may see your good deeds and glorify your Father in heaven."**

We ask for Your protection and guidance as we journey from here. Keep us safe from harm and lead us in the paths of righteousness. As it is written in **Psalm 23:3, "He guides me along the right paths for his name's sake."**

Lord, may the prayers we've lifted up today continue to echo in our hearts and in the world around us. Let Your kingdom come and Your will be done in our lives and in the lives of those we've prayed for.

As it is written in **Matthew 6:10, "Your kingdom come, your will be done, on earth as it is in heaven."**

We commit ourselves into Your hands, trusting in Your unfailing love and faithfulness. May Your peace, which surpasses all understanding, guard our hearts and minds in Christ Jesus.

As it is written in **Philippians 4:7, "And the peace of God, which transcends all understanding, will guard your hearts and your minds in Christ Jesus."**

In Jesus' name we pray,
Amen.

Prayer for Confession

Heavenly Father,

I come before You with a heavy heart, acknowledging my sins and shortcomings. Your Word teaches us in **1 John 1:9** that if we confess our sins, You are faithful and just to forgive us and to cleanse us from all unrighteousness. So, Lord, I confess my sins to You now.

Forgive me, Father, for the times when I have strayed from Your path, for the thoughts, words, and deeds that have not brought glory to Your name. I confess any pride, selfishness, anger, or bitterness that has taken root in my heart. I ask for Your forgiveness for the times when I have failed to love You with all my heart, soul, mind, and strength, and to love my neighbor as myself, as You have instructed in **Matthew 22:37-39.**

Lord, I confess my sins of omission on the good deeds I have failed to do, the opportunities I have missed to serve others and to be a light in the world. It's clearly mentioned in **Proverbs 3:5-6**, that we must **"Trust in the Lord with all your heart and lean not on your own understanding; in all your ways submit to him, and he will make your paths straight"**. Forgive me for the times when I have neglected to seek Your guidance and wisdom, relying instead on my own understanding.

I confess, Father, that I am in need of Your mercy and grace. I thank You for the sacrifice of Your Son, Jesus Christ, who died on the cross to pay the penalty for my sins. By His blood, I am redeemed and made righteous in Your sight as mentioned in **Romans 5:8-9**. Thank You for Your unfailing love and forgiveness.

Help me, Lord, to turn away from my sins and to walk in obedience to Your word. As I read in **Psalm 51:10, "Create in me a pure heart, O God, and renew a steadfast spirit within me."** Fill me with Your Holy Spirit, that I may live a life that is pleasing to You.

Thank You, Father, for hearing my prayer and for Your abundant mercy and grace. May my confession lead to true repentance and transformation, as I seek to follow You with all my heart.

In Jesus' name, I pray,
Amen.

Prayer for Compassion

Heavenly Father,

I come before You with a heart filled with gratitude for Your boundless compassion towards us. Your Word teaches us in **Lamentations 3:22-23** that Your mercies are new every morning, and Your compassion never fails. Thank You for Your steadfast love that endures forever.

Lord, You are the ultimate example of compassion. In **Matthew 9:36**, it is written that when Jesus saw the crowds, he had compassion on them because they were harassed and helpless, like sheep without a shepherd. I pray that You would fill my heart with the same compassion that Jesus had, so that I may see others through Your eyes of love and extend a helping hand to those in need.

Father, Your Word instructs us in **Colossians 3:12** to clothe ourselves with compassion, kindness, humility, gentleness, and patience. I ask that You would help me to cultivate a spirit of compassion in my daily life, so that I may reflect Your character to those around me.

Lord, You have called us to love our neighbors as ourselves. In **Luke 10:33-34**, Jesus told the parable of the Good Samaritan, who showed compassion to a wounded stranger. May I follow the example of the Good Samaritan, reaching out to those who are hurting and in need, regardless of their background or circumstances.

Father, I pray for the grace to extend compassion not only to those who are easy to love, but also to those who may have wronged me or caused me pain. Help me to forgive as You have forgiven me, and to show compassion even to my enemies, just as Jesus did on the cross.

May Your compassion flow through me, Lord, touching the lives of those I encounter and bringing healing and hope to a broken world.

In Jesus' name, I pray,
Amen.

Prayer for
Dream Big: Setting High Goals

Heavenly Father,

We come before You with hearts full of excitement and anticipation for the dreams and visions You have placed within us. Your word tells us in **Jeremiah 29:11, "For I know the plans I have for you," declares the Lord, "plans to prosper you and not to harm you, plans to give you hope and a future."** We thank You, Lord, for the dreams that stir our hearts and inspire us to pursue Your purposes for our lives.

Father, we acknowledge that our biggest dreams are often beyond our own understanding and abilities. Yet we know that nothing is impossible with You. As it says in **Ephesians 3:20, "Now to Him who is able to do immeasurably more than all we ask or imagine, according to His power that is at work within us."**

We surrender our goals and dreams into Your hands, trusting that You will fulfill them according to Your perfect will and timing. Give us the faith to step out in obedience and pursue the dreams You have placed within us, knowing that You are faithful to fulfill Your promises.

Grant us the wisdom and discernment to recognize the opportunities and challenges that come with pursuing our dreams. Help us to remain steadfast in faith, even when the path seems uncertain or difficult.

We pray that our dreams would not only bring fulfillment and joy to our lives but also glorify Your name and advance Your kingdom on earth. May our dreams be aligned with Your purposes and bring about transformation in our lives and in the lives of those around us.

Lord, we commit our lives into Your loving hands, trusting that You will bring them to fruition for Your glory. May we never lose sight of the incredible plans You have for us, and may we walk boldly in faith as we pursue the dreams You have placed within us.

In Jesus' name, we pray,
Amen.

Prayer for
Contentment

Heavenly Father,

I come before You today with a heart filled with gratitude for all the blessings You have bestowed upon me. Your Word teaches us in **Philippians 4:11-13** that we can find contentment in every situation through Christ who gives us strength. I pray that You would help me to cultivate a spirit of contentment in my life, regardless of my circumstances.

Lord, forgive me for the times when I have allowed discontentment to creep into my heart. Help me to focus on the abundance of blessings that surround me, rather than dwelling on what I lack. Teach me to be content with what I have, knowing that true contentment comes from You alone.

Father, Your Word tells us in **1 Timothy 6:6** that godliness with contentment is great gain. I pray that You would help me to prioritize godliness in my life, seeking first Your kingdom and Your righteousness. May I find my greatest satisfaction and fulfillment in knowing and serving You.

Lord, guard my heart against the temptations of this world, and the desires of the flesh, which promise fulfillment but ultimately leave us empty and dissatisfied. Help me to resist the urge to chase after material possessions, status, or worldly success, and instead to find my identity and worth in You.

Father, I thank You for the peace that surpasses all understanding, which guards our hearts and minds in Christ Jesus as mentioned in **Philippians 4:7**. May Your peace fill me to overflowing, anchoring my soul in the midst of life's storms and uncertainties.

As mentioned in **Romans 8:28**, help me to trust in Your provision and to rest in the knowledge that You are working all things together for my good. May I find contentment in Your presence and in the assurance of Your unfailing love.

In Jesus' name, I pray,
Amen.

Prayer for
Daughter

Heavenly Father,

I come before You with a heart full of gratitude for the precious gift of my daughter, **[Daughter's Name]**, whom You have entrusted into my care. Your Word assures us in **Psalm 127:3, "Children are a heritage from the Lord, offspring a reward from him."** I thank You for the blessing she is to our family and for the joy and love she brings into our lives.

Lord, I lift up **[Daughter's Name]** to You, knowing that You have a perfect plan and purpose for her life. Your Word in **Jeremiah 29:11** reminds us, **"For I know the plans I have for you, declares the Lord, plans to prosper you and not to harm you, plans to give you hope and a future."** I pray that she may walk in the fullness of the destiny You have ordained for her.

Father, I ask for Your protection and guidance over **[Daughter's Name]**. Surround her with Your love and shield her from harm. Your Word in **Psalm 91:11** assures us, **"For he will command his angels concerning you to guard you in all your ways."** I pray that Your angels will watch over her and keep her safe wherever she goes.

Lord, I pray for **[Daughter's Name]**'s spiritual growth and relationship with You. May she come to know You personally and walk in Your ways all the days of her life. Your Word in **Proverbs 22:6** instructs us, **"Start children off on the way they should go, and even when they are old they will not turn from it."** I pray that she may grow in wisdom and stature, and in favor with You and with others.

Father, grant **[Daughter's Name]** good health, wisdom, and discernment in all her decisions. Help her to honor You in all that she does and to be a light shining brightly in this world. May she be a blessing to others and bring glory to Your name in everything she undertakes.

I commit **[Daughter's Name]** into Your loving hands, trusting in Your faithfulness and provision for her every need. May Your grace and peace be upon her now and always.

In Jesus' name, I pray,
Amen.

Prayer for
Daily Bread

Heavenly Father,

We come before You with grateful hearts, acknowledging You as the ultimate provider of all our needs. Your Word assures us in **Matthew 6:11, "Give us today our daily bread," reminding us to come to You with trust and dependence for our daily sustenance.**

Lord, we thank You for the countless blessings You provide each day, including the food we eat. Your Word declares in **Psalm 145:15-16, "The eyes of all look to you, and you give them their food at the proper time. You open your hand and satisfy the desires of every living thing."** We recognize that every good gift comes from You, and we are grateful for Your abundant provision.

Father, we pray for those who lack daily bread, whether due to poverty, famine, or other circumstances. Your Word encourages us to be compassionate and generous towards those in need, as stated in **Proverbs 22:9, "The generous will themselves be blessed, for they share their food with the poor."** May we be instruments of Your love and provision, sharing what we have with those who are hungry and in need. Lord, we ask for Your guidance and wisdom in stewarding the resources You have entrusted to us. Help us to use our blessings wisely, to be mindful of those who are less fortunate, and to seek Your kingdom above all else, as instructed in **Matthew 6:33, "But seek first his kingdom and his righteousness, and all these things will be given to you as well."**

Father, as we partake of our daily bread, both physically and spiritually, may we be reminded of Your faithfulness and provision in our lives. Your Word reminds us in **Deuteronomy 8:3, "He humbled you, causing you to hunger and then feeding you with manna, which neither you nor your ancestors had known, to teach you that man does not live on bread alone but on every word that comes from the mouth of the Lord."** May we hunger for Your Word and find true satisfaction in You.

Lord, we commit our daily needs into Your hands, trusting in Your faithfulness to provide for us according to Your riches in glory. May Your name be glorified as we acknowledge You as our Provider and sustainer of life.

In Jesus' name, we pray,
Amen.

Prayer for
Dedication to Ministry

Heavenly Father,

I come before You with a humble heart, recognizing Your authority and Your perfect plan for my life. Your word in **Isaiah 6:8** reminds me of the prophet Isaiah's response when he heard Your voice saying, "Whom shall I send, and who will go for us?" Isaiah responded, "Here I am! Send me."

Lord, like Isaiah, I desire to be used by You for Your glory and Your kingdom purposes. I surrender myself completely to Your will and Your leading. Use me as Your instrument to spread Your love, truth, and grace to those around me.

Father, I also draw inspiration from the apostle Paul's words in **2 Timothy 2:21**, where he encourages us to be vessels for honorable use, set apart as holy, useful to the Master, ready for every good work. May my life be set apart for Your purposes, ready and available for whatever task You have prepared for me.

Help me to walk in obedience to Your word, following the example of Jesus Christ, who said in **John 4:34, "My food is to do the will of him who sent me and to finish his work."** May my greatest joy be found in doing Your will and fulfilling Your purposes.

Lord, I ask for Your guidance and empowerment as I step out in faith to serve You. Fill me afresh with Your Holy Spirit, equipping me with everything I need to fulfill Your calling on my life.

Thank You, Lord, for the privilege of being used by You. May my life bring glory and honor to Your name and may Your kingdom purposes be advanced through me.

In Jesus' name, I pray,
Amen.

Prayer for Depression

Heavenly Father,

In moments of deep despair and darkness, we come before You, seeking Your light and hope to shine upon us. Your Word assures us in **Psalm 34:18** that **"The Lord is close to the brokenhearted and saves those who are crushed in spirit."** We cling to this promise, knowing that even in our darkest moments, You are with us. Lord, we lift up to You those who are struggling with depression. We ask for Your healing touch to penetrate the depths of their souls and bring restoration to their minds and hearts. Your Word declares in **Psalm 30:2, "Lord my God, I called to you for help, and you healed me."** We cry out to You now, trusting in Your unfailing love and compassion.

Father, we ask for Your peace that surpasses all understanding to guard their hearts and minds in Christ Jesus as mentioned in **Philippians 4:7**. As we read in **1 Peter 5:7**, help them to cast all their anxieties on You, knowing that You care for them.

Lord, we pray for strength and perseverance for those battling depression. Your Word reminds us in **Isaiah 40:31** that **"but those who hope in the Lord will renew their strength. They will soar on wings like eagles; they will run and not grow weary, they will walk and not be faint."** May they find renewed strength and hope in You, trusting in Your faithfulness to sustain them.

Father, we ask for Your wisdom and guidance for those supporting and caring for loved ones struggling with depression. Help them to offer comfort, understanding, and encouragement, pointing their loved ones to Your unfailing love and grace. Lord, we pray for breakthroughs and miracles in the lives of those battling depression. Your Word proclaims in **Jeremiah 29:11, "For I know the plans I have for you," declares the Lord, "plans to prosper you and not to harm you, plans to give you hope and a future."** May they cling to the hope found in You, knowing that You have a purpose and a plan for their lives.

Father, we surrender all our burdens and cares into Your loving hands, trusting in Your promise to carry us through every trial and tribulation. May Your peace reign in our hearts and Your light shine in the midst of darkness.

In Jesus' name, we pray,
Amen.

Prayer for
Disruptions

Heavenly Father,

In moments of disappointment and uncertainty, I come before You, acknowledging Your sovereignty over all things. Your word assures us in **Proverbs 19:21, "Many are the plans in a person's heart, but it is the Lord's purpose that prevails."** Help me to trust in Your divine plan, even when my own plans seem to falter.

Lord, I confess my feelings of frustration and confusion when things don't go as I had hoped or expected. Yet, I know that Your ways are higher than my ways, and Your thoughts are higher than my thoughts as written in **Isaiah 55:8-9**. Help me to surrender my desires and ambitions to Your perfect will.

Father, I pray for Your peace to fill my heart in the midst of disappointment. Your word reminds us in **Philippians 4:6-7, "Do not be anxious about anything, but in every situation, by prayer and petition, with thanksgiving, present your requests to God. And the peace of God, which transcends all understanding, will guard your hearts and your minds in Christ Jesus."** Grant me Your peace that surpasses all understanding, anchoring my soul in Your unchanging love.

Lord, I ask for Your wisdom to discern the lessons and opportunities hidden within setbacks and obstacles. Your word assures us in **Romans 8:28, "And we know that in all things God works for the good of those who love him, who have been called according to his purpose."** Help me to see beyond my immediate circumstances and to trust in Your redemptive power.

Father, I surrender my disappointments and failures into Your hands, knowing that You are able to turn even the darkest situations into blessings. Your word declares in **Jeremiah 29:11, "For I know the plans I have for you," declares the Lord, "plans to prosper you and not to harm you, plans to give you hope and a future."** Strengthen my faith and renew my hope in Your unfailing promises.

Lord, may my response to disappointment be one of faith, gratitude, and perseverance. Help me to remain steadfast in prayer and to trust in Your faithfulness, knowing that You are working all things together for my good and Your glory.

In Jesus' name, I pray,
Amen.

Prayer for Discipline

Heavenly Father,

We come before You acknowledging Your wisdom and sovereignty over our lives. Your Word teaches us in **Proverbs 3:11-12, "My son, do not despise the Lord's discipline, and do not resent his rebuke, because the Lord disciplines those he loves, as a father the son he delights in."**

Lord, we recognize that discipline is a sign of Your love for us, a means by which You shape and mold us into the image of Your Son, Jesus Christ. Help us to embrace Your discipline with humility and obedience, knowing that it is for our good and growth in faith. Give us the strength and self-control to resist temptation and walk in righteousness. Your Word reminds us in **1 Corinthians 9:27, "No, I strike a blow to my body and make it my slave so that after I have preached to others, I myself will not be disqualified for the prize."** Grant us the discipline to pursue holiness and to flee from sin.

Father, we pray for discipline in our spiritual lives, that we may be diligent in prayer, studying Your Word, and living out our faith daily. Your Word instructs us in **2 Timothy 3:16-17, "All Scripture is God-breathed and is useful for teaching, rebuking, correcting and training in righteousness, so that the servant of God may be thoroughly equipped for every good work."** Help us to be disciplined students of Your Word, growing in knowledge and wisdom.

Lord, we also pray for discipline in our relationships, that we may speak words of kindness and encouragement, and demonstrate love and forgiveness. Your Word admonishes us in **Ephesians 4:29, "Do not let any unwholesome talk come out of your mouths, but only what is helpful for building others up according to their needs, that it may benefit those who listen."** Grant us the discipline to build up others and to live in harmony with one another.

Help us to be disciplined stewards of our time, talents, and resources, using them wisely for Your kingdom purposes. Your Word teaches us in **Colossians 3:23-24, "Whatever you do, work at it with all your heart, as working for the Lord, not for human masters, since you know that you will receive an inheritance from the Lord as a reward. It is the Lord Christ you are serving."** May we be faithful and disciplined servants, serving You wholeheartedly in all that we do. Lord, we surrender our lives to Your loving discipline, trusting in Your faithfulness and goodness. Help us to persevere in discipline, knowing that it produces a harvest of righteousness and peace for those who are trained by it as mentioned in **Hebrews 12:11.**

In Jesus' name, we pray,
Amen.

Prayer for
Emergencies

Heavenly Father,

In this moment of emergency, I turn to You, knowing that You are my refuge and strength, always ready to help in times of trouble as mentioned in **Psalm 46:1**. I trust in Your sovereignty and Your ability to intervene in this situation according to Your perfect will.

Lord, Your Word assures us in **Psalm 50:15** that when we call upon You in the day of trouble, You will deliver us and honor us. I lift up this emergency to You, knowing that You are able to bring about a resolution that is in accordance with Your divine plan.

Father, I pray for Your protection and provision over all those who are involved in this emergency. Surround them with Your angels, guarding them from harm and guiding them to safety. As it is mentioned in **Psalm 91:11-12, "For he will command his angels concerning you to guard you in all your ways; they will lift you up in their hands, so that you will not strike your foot against a stone."**

Lord, I ask for wisdom and discernment for those who are in positions of authority and responsibility in handling this emergency. May they be guided by Your Spirit in making decisions that will lead to the best possible outcome.

Father, I also pray for peace and comfort for those who are affected by this emergency. May they feel Your presence in the midst of fear and uncertainty, trusting in Your promise to never leave us nor forsake us as mentioned in **Deuteronomy 31:6.**

Lord, I commit this emergency into Your hands, knowing that You are able to work all things together for good for those who love You and are called according to Your purpose, as written in **Romans 8:28**.

In Jesus' name, I pray,
Amen.

Prayer for Earth and Universe

Heavenly Father,

We come before You with hearts filled with awe and reverence for the magnificent creation You have entrusted to us. Your Word declares in **Psalm 24:1, "The earth is the Lord's, and everything in it, the world, and all who live in it."** We acknowledge Your sovereignty over the entire universe and offer our prayers for the care and preservation of Your creation.

Lord, we recognize the beauty and diversity of the earth and the universe, which reflect Your glory and majesty. Your Word proclaims in **Psalm 19:1, "The heavens declare the glory of God; the skies proclaim the work of his hands."** We thank You for the wonders of creation, from the vastness of the galaxies to the intricacy of the smallest living organisms.

Father, we confess that humanity has not always been good stewards of the earth and its resources. We have exploited and polluted Your creation, causing harm to the environment and endangering the delicate balance of ecosystems. Forgive us, Lord, and help us to repent and turn from our ways, as Your Word instructs us in **2 Chronicles 7:14, "If my people, who are called by my name, will humble themselves and pray and seek my face and turn from their wicked ways, then I will hear from heaven, and I will forgive their sin and will heal their land."**

Grant us, O Lord, wisdom and understanding to care for the earth and all living creatures. Help us to be responsible stewards of Your creation, using its resources wisely and with respect for future generations. Your Word teaches us in **Genesis 2:15, "The Lord God took the man and put him in the Garden of Eden to work it and take care of it." May we fulfill this mandate with diligence and love.**

Father, we lift up to You those who are suffering from the effects of environmental degradation, including natural disasters, pollution, and climate change. Your Word assures us in **Isaiah 41:10, "So do not fear, for I am with you; do not be dismayed, for I am your God. I will strengthen you and help you; I will uphold you with my righteous right hand."** Comfort and protect them, O Lord, and grant them hope for the future.

We pray for leaders and policymakers around the world, that they may make decisions that prioritize the well-being of the earth and its inhabitants. Your Word exhorts us in **Proverbs 11:14, "For lack of guidance a nation falls, but victory is won through many advisers."** Guide them in their efforts to promote sustainability and environmental justice. Lord, we commit the earth and the universe into Your loving hands, trusting in Your providence and grace. May Your creation continue to declare Your glory and testify to Your goodness for generations to come.

In Jesus' name, we pray,
Amen.

Prayer for
End of Violence and War

Heavenly Father,

We come before You with heavy hearts, grieving over the violence and conflicts that plague our world. Your Word teaches us in **Matthew 5:9, "Blessed are the peacemakers, for they will be called children of God."** We pray earnestly for Your peace to reign in the hearts of all people and for an end to violence and war. Lord, You are the Prince of Peace, and Your desire is for all nations to dwell in harmony and unity. We lift up to You the regions torn apart by conflict and strife, asking for Your intervention and reconciliation. Your Word declares in **Psalm 46:9, "He makes wars cease to the ends of the earth. He breaks the bow and shatters the spear; he burns the shields with fire."** We pray for Your divine intervention to bring an end to all wars and conflicts, replacing them with Your peace that surpasses all understanding.

Father, we pray for the leaders of nations, asking for Your wisdom and guidance as they navigate complex geopolitical issues. Help them to seek justice, promote reconciliation, and prioritize the well-being of their people above all else. Your Word instructs us in **Proverbs 21:1, "In the Lord's hand the king's heart is a stream of water that he channels toward all who please him."** We trust in Your sovereignty to guide and direct the hearts of world leaders towards paths of peace and righteousness. Lord, we also lift up to You all those who are victims of violence and war – the innocent civilians, the displaced refugees, and the courageous men and women serving in the military. Your Word assures us in **Psalm 34:18, "The Lord is close to the brokenhearted and saves those who are crushed in spirit."** We ask for Your comfort and protection to surround them, providing refuge and strength in the midst of turmoil.

Father, we pray for hearts to be transformed by Your love and grace, leading to reconciliation and forgiveness among enemies. Your Word teaches us in **Romans 12:18, "If it is possible, as far as it depends on you, live at peace with everyone."** May Your Spirit work in the hearts of individuals and communities, fostering forgiveness, understanding, and compassion. Lord, we commit the cause of peace into Your hands, knowing that You are the ultimate source of peace and reconciliation. Your Word proclaims in **Isaiah 2:4, "He will judge between the nations and will settle disputes for many peoples. They will beat their swords into plowshares and their spears into pruning hooks. Nation will not take up sword against nation, nor will they train for war anymore."** We eagerly await the fulfillment of Your promise when Your kingdom of peace will reign forevermore.

In Jesus' name, we pray,
Amen.

Prayer for
End of Abortion

Heavenly Father,

We come before You with heavy hearts, grieving over the millions of lives lost to abortion and the deep wounds it inflicts upon our society. Your word teaches us in **Psalm 139:13-16** that You knit each person together in their mother's womb, and that every life is precious and valuable in Your sight. Lord, we pray for an end to the scourge of abortion. Give us the courage to speak up for those who cannot speak for themselves, as instructed in **Proverbs 31:8-9**. Help us to be a voice for the voiceless, advocating for the protection of innocent unborn children and offering support and alternatives to those facing unplanned pregnancies.

Father, we pray for those who have been affected by abortion, whether as mothers, fathers, or family members. Comfort them in their pain and guilt, and lead them to the healing and forgiveness found in Jesus Christ. Your word assures us in **1 John 1:9** that if we confess our sins, You are faithful and just to forgive us our sins and to cleanse us from all unrighteousness.

We pray for lawmakers and leaders, that they may enact laws and policies that uphold the sanctity of life from conception to natural death. Open their eyes to the humanity of the unborn and grant them the wisdom and compassion to protect and defend the most vulnerable members of society.

Lord, we lift up organizations and individuals who are working tirelessly to provide support, resources, and education to mothers and families facing crisis pregnancies. Bless their efforts and multiply their impact, that more lives may be saved and transformed by Your grace.

Father, we know that ultimately, the battle against abortion is a spiritual one. Help us to fight not only with earthly weapons but with the spiritual weapons You have provided, as stated in **Ephesians 6:12**. Empower us with Your Holy Spirit to pray fervently, to intercede for the unborn and their families, and to engage in spiritual warfare against the forces of darkness that promote and perpetuate abortion.

Lord, we cling to the promise of **Isaiah 61:1** that You have sent Jesus to bind up the brokenhearted and to proclaim liberty to the captives. May Your kingdom come and Your will be done on earth as it is in heaven, where every life is cherished and protected.

In Jesus' name, we pray,
Amen.

Prayer for
Engagement Couples

Heavenly Father,

We come before You with hearts full of joy and gratitude as we celebrate the love and commitment of **[Couple's Names]** who have chosen to embark on this journey of engagement together. Thank You for bringing them into each other's lives and for the bond of love that unites them. As it is written in **Ecclesiastes 4:9-10, "Two are better than one, because they have a good return for their labor: If either of them falls down, one can help the other up. But pity anyone who falls and has no one to help them up."**

Lord, we pray for **[Couple's Names]** as they prepare to enter into the covenant of marriage. May their love continue to deepen and grow stronger with each passing day. Grant them wisdom, patience, and understanding as they navigate the joys and challenges of planning their future together. As it is written in **Proverbs 19:14, "Houses and wealth are inherited from parents, but a prudent wife is from the Lord."**

Bless their relationship, O Lord, and may it be grounded in Your love and guided by Your principles. Help **[Couple's Names]** to build a foundation of faith, trust, and mutual respect that will sustain them through every season of life. As it is written in **Colossians 3:14, "And over all these virtues put on love, which binds them all together in perfect unity."** Lord, we also lift up their families and loved ones who rejoice with them in this special time. May they offer support, encouragement, and wisdom as **[Couple's Names]** prepare for marriage. As it is written in **1 Thessalonians 5:11, "Therefore encourage one another and build each other up, just as in fact you are doing."**

As they journey towards their wedding day, may they keep their eyes fixed on You, the author and perfecter of their faith. May they seek Your guidance in all their decisions and rely on Your strength to overcome any obstacles they may face. As it is written in **Proverbs 3:5-6, "Trust in the Lord with all your heart and lean not on your own understanding; in all your ways submit to him, and he will make your paths straight."** We pray for a lifetime of blessings upon **[Couple's Names]**. May their marriage be a reflection of Your love and grace, bringing glory to Your name and joy to their hearts.

In Jesus' name we pray,
Amen.

Prayer for
Enemies

Heavenly Father,

I come before You with a heavy heart, knowing that You have called us to love even our enemies, as Jesus taught us in **Matthew 5:44**. Lord, I confess that it is difficult for me to pray for those who have hurt me or who consider themselves my enemies, but I know that Your love transcends human understanding, and You desire reconciliation and peace among all people.

Father, I lift up my enemies to You now. I pray that You would soften their hearts and open their eyes to Your truth and love. Help them to see the error of their ways and to turn from their wickedness. May they come to experience the transforming power of Your grace and mercy in their lives. Lord, I release any feelings of anger, bitterness, or resentment towards my enemies, and I ask for Your help in forgiving them, as You have forgiven me. As instructed in **Ephesians 4:32**, help us remember to **"Be kind and compassionate to one another, forgiving each other, just as in Christ God forgave you."**

Fill my heart with Your love, compassion, and understanding towards them, and help me to respond to their hostility with kindness and patience.

Father, I pray for reconciliation and healing in our relationship. Help us to overcome our differences and to find common ground. Give us the wisdom and humility to seek peace and pursue it, as Your Word instructs us in **Psalm 34:14**.

Lord, I surrender my enemies into Your hands, trusting in Your justice and righteousness. May Your will be done in their lives, and may they come to know the depth of Your love and forgiveness. Thank You, Lord, for Your grace that covers us all. May Your love triumph over hatred and division, and may Your kingdom come and Your will be done on earth as it is in heaven.

In Jesus' name, I pray,
Amen.

Prayer for
Exams

Heavenly Father,

As I prepare to take this exam, I come before You with a heart full of trust and dependence on Your wisdom and guidance. Your Word tells us in **James 1:5, "If any of you lacks wisdom, you should ask God, who gives generously to all without finding fault, and it will be given to you."**

Lord, I ask for Your wisdom to fill my mind as I study and review. Help me to understand and retain the information I need to succeed. Give me clarity of thought and focus as I prepare for this exam.

I pray for Your peace to guard my heart and calm any anxiety or fear that may arise. Your Word assures us in **Philippians 4:6-7, "Do not be anxious about anything, but in every situation, by prayer and petition, with thanksgiving, present your requests to God. And the peace of God, which transcends all understanding, will guard your hearts and your minds in Christ Jesus."**

Lord, I trust in Your promise to be with me every step of the way. Your Word also reminds us in **Joshua 1:9, "Have I not commanded you? Be strong and courageous. Do not be afraid; do not be discouraged, for the Lord your God will be with you wherever you go."**

I commit this exam into Your hands, knowing that You are in control of the outcome. Help me to do my best and to glorify You in all that I do. May Your will be done in my life, and may I honor You with my efforts and achievements.

In Jesus' name I pray,
Amen.

Prayer for
Events or Parties

Heavenly Father,

We gather before You today with hearts full of anticipation and excitement as we prepare for this upcoming event. Your Word reminds us in **Proverbs 16:3, "Commit to the Lord whatever you do, and he will establish your plans."** We come before You, committing this event into Your hands and seeking Your guidance and blessing upon it.

Lord, we thank You for the opportunity to come together in fellowship and celebration. We pray that this event will be successful according to Your will and purpose. May it be a time of joy, unity, and inspiration for all who attend.

Father, we ask for Your wisdom and discernment as we make final preparations. Guide us in our planning, decision-making, and execution of every detail. Your Word instructs us in **James 1:5, "If any of you lacks wisdom, you should ask God, who gives generously to all without finding fault, and it will be given to you."** We humbly ask for Your wisdom to be poured out upon us.

Lord, we pray for Your presence to be felt throughout the event. May Your Spirit move among us, touching hearts and transforming lives. Help us to glorify You in all that we say and do, reflecting Your love and grace to those around us.

Father, we also lift up all the attendees of this event. May they feel welcomed, valued, and inspired by what takes place. Open their hearts to receive whatever messages, lessons, or experiences You have in store for them.

Lord, we commit this event into Your hands, trusting in Your sovereignty and provision. May it bring honor and glory to Your name and fulfill the purposes You have ordained for it.

In Jesus' name we pray,
Amen.

Prayer for Faith

Heavenly Father,

I come before You today with a heart full of faith, trusting in Your promises and Your faithfulness. Your Word tells me in **Hebrews 11:1**, that faith is the assurance of things hoped for, the conviction of things not seen, and I thank You for the gift of faith that You have given me.

Lord, I pray that You would increase my faith, that I may walk boldly and confidently in Your will. Help me to trust in You with all my heart and not lean on my own understanding, acknowledging You in all my ways so that You may direct my paths as instructed in **Proverbs 3:5-6**.

Father, I thank You for the examples of faith found in Your Word, such as Abraham, who believed You even when circumstances seemed impossible, and it was credited to him as righteousness as mentioned in **Genesis 15:6**. Like him, may my faith in You be unwavering, knowing that nothing is too difficult for You.

Lord Jesus, as mentioned in **Hebrews 12:2**, You are the author and perfecter of our faith, and I look to You as the source of my strength and confidence. Help me to fix my eyes on You, the one who is faithful and true, and to walk by faith, not by sight as written in **2 Corinthians 5:7**.

Holy Spirit, I invite You to fill me afresh with Your presence and power, empowering me to live a life that honors You and brings glory to Your name. May my faith be active and alive, producing fruit that will last for eternity as mentioned in **James 2:17**.

Thank You, Lord, for hearing my prayer and for the assurance that nothing is impossible for those who believe as You have mentioned in **Mark 9:23**. Strengthen my faith, O God, and help me to trust in You more deeply each day.

In Jesus' name, I pray,
Amen.

Prayer for
Facing Difficult Decisions

Heavenly Father,

We come before You with hearts burdened by the weight of difficult decisions, seeking Your wisdom and guidance in the midst of uncertainty. Your word reminds us in **James 1:5, "If any of you lacks wisdom, you should ask God, who gives generously to all without finding fault, and it will be given to you."**

Lord, we acknowledge Your sovereignty over all things, and we trust in Your perfect plan for our lives. As we face these challenging decisions, we seek Your wisdom, knowing that You alone have the answers we need.

Father, grant us clarity of mind and discernment of spirit as we consider our options. Help us to see beyond the immediate circumstances and to discern Your will for our lives. Your word assures us in **Proverbs 3:5-6, "Trust in the Lord with all your heart and lean not on your own understanding; in all your ways submit to him, and he will make your paths straight."**

Lord, we surrender these decisions into Your hands, trusting that You will lead us in the way that is best for us. Give us peace in the midst of uncertainty, knowing that You are with us every step of the way.

Father, we pray for the courage to follow Your leading, even when it may seem difficult or uncertain. Your word promises in **Isaiah 30:21, "Whether you turn to the right or to the left, your ears will hear a voice behind you, saying, "This is the way; walk in it."**

Lord, help us to trust in Your providence and to walk by faith, knowing that You are working all things together for our good as mentioned in **Romans 8:28**. Give us the strength to step out in obedience, trusting that Your hand is guiding and directing our steps.

Father, we thank You for Your faithfulness and Your unfailing love toward us. May Your wisdom guide our decisions and Your peace guard our hearts as we seek to honor You in all that we do.

In Jesus' name, we pray,
Amen.

Prayer for
Fasting

Heavenly Father,

As I embark on this time of fasting and seeking Your face, I am reminded of the words of Jesus in **Matthew 6:16-18**, where He teaches us about the importance of fasting with sincerity and humility. Lord, I come before You with a humble heart, seeking Your presence and guidance during this time of spiritual discipline.

Your Word teaches us in **Isaiah 58:6-7** about the kind of fasting that pleases You: **"Is not this the kind of fasting I have chosen: to loose the chains of injustice and untie the cords of the yoke, to set the oppressed free and break every yoke? Is it not to share your food with the hungry and to provide the poor wanderer with shelter—when you see the naked, to clothe them, and not to turn away from your own flesh and blood?"**

Father, as I fast, help me to focus not only on abstaining from food but also on drawing closer to You and aligning my heart with Your will. Show me areas of my life where I need to break free from bondage, whether it be sin, unhealthy habits, or distractions that hinder my relationship with You.

May this time of fasting be a catalyst for spiritual breakthrough and renewal in my life. Help me to deepen my prayer life, to seek Your wisdom and guidance, and to intercede for others who are in need.

Lord, as I deny myself physical nourishment, fill me with Your spiritual sustenance. Your Word tells us in **Matthew 4:4** that **"Man shall not live on bread alone, but on every word that comes from the mouth of God."** May I hunger and thirst for Your righteousness, finding true satisfaction and fulfillment in You alone.

I surrender my desires, my weaknesses, and my burdens to You, trusting in Your strength to sustain me through this fast. Give me the endurance and perseverance to press on, knowing that You are with me every step of the way.

May this time of fasting be pleasing in Your sight, O Lord, and may it bring glory to Your name. As I seek You with all my heart, may I experience a deeper intimacy with You and a greater understanding of Your love and grace.

In Jesus' name, I pray,
Amen.

Prayer for
Family

Heavenly Father,

We come before You as a family, united in love and faith, seeking Your presence and blessings upon our lives. As it is written in **Psalm 133:1, "How good and pleasant it is when God's people live together in unity!"**

Lord, we thank You for the gift of family. We pray for unity among us, that our bonds may be strengthened, and our relationships deepened. Help us to love one another as You have loved us, to forgive one another as You have forgiven us, and to support one another in times of joy and in times of need. As it is written in **Colossians 3:13, "Bear with each other and forgive one another if any of You has a grievance against someone. Forgive as the Lord forgave you."**

Father, we lift up our health to You. Grant us the strength and energy in our bodies, minds, and spirits. Heal any sickness or pain that is affecting us, and give us the wisdom to care for our bodies as temples of Your Holy Spirit. As it is written in **3 John 1:2, "Dear friend, I pray that you may enjoy good health and that all may go well with you, even as your soul is getting along well."**

We also bring our desires for prosperity before You, knowing that You are the provider of all good things. Bless the work of our hands and the endeavors of our hearts. Grant us success and prosperity in all that we do, that we may be a blessing to others and glorify Your name. As it is written in **Deuteronomy 8:18, "But remember the Lord your God, for it is he who gives you the ability to produce wealth."**

Lord, we recognize that true prosperity comes from knowing You and walking in Your ways. Help us to seek first Your kingdom and Your righteousness, trusting that all these things will be added unto us. As You have mentioned in **Matthew 6:33, "But seek first the kingdom of God and his righteousness, and all these things will be added to you."**

May Your presence dwell in our home, filling it with peace, joy, and Your abundant blessings. Guide us in the paths of righteousness, and may our lives be a testimony to Your goodness and grace.

In Jesus' name we pray,
Amen.

Prayer for Fear

Heavenly Father,

I come before You with a heart burdened by fear, knowing that You are the only one who can truly bring peace and calmness to my soul. Your Word tells me not to fear, for You are with me; not to be dismayed, for You are my God. You will strengthen me and help me; You will uphold me with Your righteous right hand as written in **Isaiah 41:10**.

Lord, I confess that fear has gripped my heart and mind, causing me to doubt Your goodness and Your power. But Your Word in **2 Timothy 1:7**, reminds me that You have not given me a spirit of fear, but of power, love, and a sound mind. Help me to claim this truth and to walk in the confidence of Your promises.

Father, I surrender my fears to You, the fear of the unknown, the fear of failure, the fear of rejection, and all other fears that weigh heavy on my heart. Replace them with Your perfect love, which casts out all fear. As written in **1 John 4:18, "There is no fear in love. But perfect love drives out fear, because fear has to do with punishment. The one who fears is not made perfect in love."**

Lord, when I am afraid, help me to trust in You. Remind me that You are my refuge and strength, an ever-present help in times of trouble as written in **Psalm 46:1**. Teach me to turn to You in prayer and to seek Your peace that surpasses all understanding. As mentioned in **Philippians 4:6-7, "Do not be anxious about anything, but in every situation, by prayer and petition, with thanksgiving, present your requests to God. And the peace of God, which transcends all understanding, will guard your hearts and your minds in Christ Jesus."**

Father, I pray for the courage to face my fears with faith, knowing that You are greater than anything I may encounter. Give me the strength to stand firm in Your promises and to walk boldly in the path You have set before me.

Lord, I thank You for Your faithfulness and Your unfailing love. Help me to trust in You with all my heart and to lean not on my own understanding, knowing that You will direct my paths as written in **Proverbs 3:5-6**.

In Jesus' name, I pray,
Amen.

Prayer for
Father

Heavenly Father,

I come before You today with a heart full of gratitude for the gift of my father, *[Father's Name]*. Thank You for his love, guidance, and presence in my life. I lift him up to You now, knowing that You are the source of all strength and comfort. As it is written in **Psalm 28:7, "The Lord is my strength and my shield; my heart trusts in him, and he helps me. My heart leaps for joy, and with my song I praise him."**

Lord, I pray for my father's health and well-being. Grant him strength and vitality in his body, mind, and spirit. Surround him with Your healing presence, and may any ailments or concerns be eased by Your touch. As it is written in **Psalm 41:3, "The Lord sustains them on their sickbed and restores them from their bed of illness."** Father, I also pray for my father's spiritual journey. Draw him closer to You each day, deepening his faith and trust in Your goodness and love. May he find peace and purpose in knowing You and following Your will for his life. As it is written in **James 4:8, "Come near to God and he will come near to you."**

Guide my father in his roles and responsibilities as a husband, father, and provider. Give him wisdom and discernment in decision-making, and help him to lead our family with grace and integrity. As it is written in **Proverbs 3:5-6, "Trust in the Lord with all your heart and lean not on your own understanding; in all your ways submit to him, and he will make your paths straight."**

Lord, I ask for Your protection over my father, both physically and spiritually. Guard him against harm and keep him safe from the schemes of the enemy. Surround him with Your angels and cover him with Your peace. As it is written in **Psalm 91:11-12, "For he will command his angels concerning you to guard you in all your ways; they will lift you up in their hands, so that you will not strike your foot against a stone."**

As I honor my father today, I thank You for the ways he has shaped me and influenced my life. May he feel deeply loved and appreciated, not just today but every day. I commit my father into Your loving hands, trusting in Your faithfulness to watch over him and to guide him in all his ways.

In Jesus' name I pray,
Amen.

Prayer for Forgiveness

Heavenly Father,

We come before You humbly, recognizing our need for Your forgiveness and grace. Your Word in **1 John 1:9** assures us, **"If we confess our sins, he is faithful and just and will forgive us our sins and purify us from all unrighteousness."** We confess our sins to You now, knowing that You are faithful to forgive and cleanse us. Lord, we acknowledge our transgressions and the ways in which we have fallen short of Your glory. We have sinned against You and others in our thoughts, words, and actions. Your Word in **Psalm 51:2-3** reminds us, **"Wash away all my iniquity and cleanse me from my sin. For I know my transgressions, and my sin is always before me."** We ask for Your mercy and forgiveness, O Lord.

We thank You for the gift of Your Son, Jesus Christ, whose sacrifice on the cross made forgiveness possible for us. Your Word in **Ephesians 1:7** declares, **"In him we have redemption through his blood, the forgiveness of sins, in accordance with the riches of God's grace."** We receive Your forgiveness with gratitude and humility, knowing that it is by Your grace alone that we are saved.

Father, we also pray for the strength to forgive those who have wronged us. Your Word in **Matthew 6:14-15** instructs us, **"For if you forgive other people when they sin against you, your heavenly Father will also forgive you. But if you do not forgive others their sins, your Father will not forgive your sins."** Help us to release bitterness and resentment from our hearts and to extend the same forgiveness to others that You have shown to us.

Lord, grant us the wisdom to learn from our mistakes and to walk in obedience to Your Word. Your Word in **Proverbs 28:13** assures us, **"Whoever conceals their sins does not prosper, but the one who confesses and renounces them finds mercy."** May we humble ourselves before You, confessing our sins and turning away from them, that we may experience the fullness of Your mercy and grace. We surrender ourselves to You, Lord, trusting in Your unfailing love and forgiveness. May Your Spirit continue to work in us, transforming us into the image of Your Son, Jesus Christ. May our lives be a testimony to Your grace and forgiveness, bringing glory to Your name.

In Jesus' name we pray,
Amen.

Prayer for
Financial Intervention

Heavenly Father,

I come before You with a humble heart, recognizing that all blessings, including financial provision, come from You. Your Word tells us in **Philippians 4:19, "And my God will meet all your needs according to the riches of his glory in Christ Jesus."** I trust in Your promise to provide for all our needs according to Your riches.

Lord, I bring before You my financial situation and ask for Your intervention. You are the God who owns everything, and nothing is impossible for You as mentioned in **Luke 1:37**. Please open the doors of provision and pour out Your blessings upon me according to Your will.

Father, Your Word also reminds us in **Matthew 6:33, "But seek first his kingdom and his righteousness, and all these things will be given to you as well."** Help me to prioritize seeking Your kingdom and righteousness above all else, trusting that You will add all things unto me, including financial provision.

Lord, I surrender my worries and anxieties about finances into Your hands, knowing that You care for me deeply as written in **1 Peter 5:7**. Grant me wisdom to manage my finances wisely and to be a good steward of the resources You entrust to me.

I pray for opportunities for increase and abundance in my finances, that I may be able to bless others and further Your kingdom work on earth. May my financial situation be a testimony to Your faithfulness and provision in my life.

Lord, I commit my financial needs into Your hands, trusting in Your provision and timing. Help me to walk by faith and not by sight, knowing that You are faithful to fulfill Your promises.

In Jesus' name I pray,
Amen.

Prayer for
Friends

Heavenly Father,

We come before You with grateful hearts for the precious gift of friendship, as Your Word declares in **Ecclesiastes 4:9-10, "Two are better than one because they have a good return for their labor: If either of them falls down, one can help the other up. But pity anyone who falls and has no one to help them up."** Thank You for the friends You have placed in our lives, who walk alongside us in both joy and sorrow. Lord, we lift up our friends to You, thanking You for the unique bond and connection we share with them. Your Word teaches us in **Proverbs 17:17, "A friend loves at all times, and a brother is born for a time of adversity."** May our friendships be grounded in love, loyalty, and mutual support, reflecting Your love for us.

Father, we pray for the well-being of our friends, both physically and spiritually. Grant them strength, peace, and wisdom as they navigate the challenges of life. Lord Jesus, we ask for Your guidance in our interactions with our friends, that we may speak words of encouragement, kindness, and truth. Your Word instructs us in **Proverbs 27:17, "As iron sharpens iron, so one person sharpens another."** May our friendships inspire growth, accountability, and spiritual edification.

Father, we pray for unity and harmony among friends, that any conflicts or misunderstandings may be resolved in Your love and grace. Your Word encourages us in **Philippians 2:2, "then make my joy complete by being like-minded, having the same love, being one in spirit and of one mind."** Help us to value and cherish the diversity of personalities and perspectives within our friendships.

Lord, we ask for Your protection over our friends, guarding them against harm, temptation, and spiritual attacks. Your Word promises in **Psalm 91:11-12, "For he will command his angels concerning you to guard you in all your ways; they will lift you up in their hands, so that you will not strike your foot against a stone."** Surround them with Your angels and cover them with Your peace.

Father, may our friendships be a reflection of Your unconditional love and grace. Help us to be faithful friends, willing to sacrificially love and serve one another, just as You have loved us. Your Word reminds us in **John 15:13, "Greater love has no one than this: to lay down one's life for one's friends."** We commit our friendships into Your loving care, trusting in Your faithfulness to strengthen, bless, and deepen the bonds of love between us. Thank You, Lord, for the precious gift of friendship, and may Your name be glorified through our relationships.

In Jesus' name, we pray,
Amen.

Prayer for Freedom

Heavenly Father,

We come before You with hearts filled with gratitude for the freedom we enjoy, both spiritually and in our earthly lives. Your word tells us in **John 8:36, "So if the Son sets you free, you will be free indeed."** We thank You, Lord, for the freedom we have through the sacrifice of Your Son, Jesus Christ.

We pray for those who are oppressed, enslaved, or imprisoned unjustly around the world. May they experience the freedom that comes from knowing You and may Your justice prevail in their situations. Your word assures us in **Isaiah 61:1, "The Spirit of the Sovereign Lord is on me, because the Lord has anointed me to proclaim good news to the poor. He has sent me to bind up the brokenhearted, to proclaim freedom for the captives and release from darkness for the prisoners."**

Father, we also ask for the freedom from the bondage of sin in our own lives. Help us to walk in the freedom and victory that comes through Christ's sacrifice on the cross. As it says in **Galatians 5:1, "It is for freedom that Christ has set us free. Stand firm, then, and do not let yourselves be burdened again by a yoke of slavery."**

Grant us the wisdom and courage to defend and uphold the freedoms that You have given us, both individually and collectively. May we use our freedom to serve one another in love, as **Galatians 5:13** reminds us, **"You, my brothers and sisters, were called to be free. But do not use your freedom to indulge the flesh; rather, serve one another humbly in love."**

We pray for the leaders of nations, that they may govern with justice and righteousness, upholding the freedoms and rights of all people. Guide them by Your Spirit to make decisions that promote peace, equality, and liberty for all.

Lord, we thank You for the precious gift of freedom, and we commit to living our lives in gratitude and obedience to You. May our lives be a reflection of Your love and grace, shining brightly in a world that longs for true freedom.

In Jesus' name, we pray,
Amen.

Prayer for
Future Spouse

Heavenly Father,

I come before You with a heart full of gratitude for Your faithfulness and goodness in my life. As I lift up my future spouse to You, I pray that You would guide and prepare both of us for the sacred union of marriage.

Lord, Your Word teaches us in **Proverbs 18:22** that he who finds a wife finds a good thing and obtains favor from the Lord. I trust in Your perfect timing and plan for our lives, knowing that You have already ordained the one who will be my future spouse.

Father, I pray for my future spouse's spiritual growth and relationship with You. May they seek You diligently, walking in Your ways and growing in faith day by day. Grant them wisdom, discernment, and a heart that is fully surrendered to Your will.

Lord, I also pray for their emotional and physical well-being. Protect them from harm and strengthen them in times of weakness as You have promised in **Isaiah 41:10**. Surround them with Your love and peace, filling their heart with joy and contentment.

Father, I pray that You would prepare us both to be selfless and loving partners in marriage. Help us to prioritize our relationship with You above all else, so that we may glorify You in our union according to **Ephesians 5:21-33**.

Lord, I commit our future marriage into Your hands, trusting in Your faithfulness to lead us and guide us every step of the way. May our love for each other be a reflection of Your unconditional love for us.

In Jesus' name, I pray,
Amen.

Prayer for Funeral or Deceased

Heavenly Father,

As we gather here today to mourn the loss of our beloved ***[Name]***, we turn to You, the God of all comfort and compassion. As written in **2 Corinthians 1:3-4, "Praise be to the God and Father of our Lord Jesus Christ, the Father of compassion and the God of all comfort, who comforts us in all our troubles, so that we can comfort those in any trouble with the comfort we ourselves receive from God."**

We thank You for the gift of ***[Name]***'s life and the impact they had on each of us. Lord, we find solace in Your promise that those who mourn will be comforted as written in **Matthew 5:4**. Wrap Your loving arms around us during this time of grief, and bring peace to our hearts as we remember the precious memories we shared with ***[Name]***.

We entrust ***[Name]***'s soul into Your care, knowing that to be absent from the body is to be present with the Lord as assured in **2 Corinthians 5:8**. May ***[Name]*** find eternal rest and joy in Your presence, where there is no more sorrow, pain, or suffering. As it is written in **Revelation 21:4, "He will wipe every tear from their eyes. There will be no more death or mourning or crying or pain, for the old order of things has passed away."**

Lord, we also pray for those who are grieving, that You would sustain them with Your strength and grant them Your peace that surpasses all understanding as mentioned in **Philippians 4:7**. Comfort them with the assurance of Your unfailing love and the hope of being reunited with ***[Name]*** in eternity.

As we celebrate ***[Name]***'s life today, help us to honor their memory by living our lives in a way that brings glory to You. May we cherish each moment and strive to love one another as You have loved us, and as instructed in **John 13:34-35**.

Finally, we thank You, Lord, for the hope we have in Jesus Christ, who conquered death and gave us the promise of eternal life. As we say goodbye to ***[Name]*** for now, we look forward to the day when we will be reunited with them in Your heavenly kingdom.

In Jesus' name, we pray,
Amen.

Prayer for Future Plans

Heavenly Father,

I come before You with hope and anticipation for the future that You have planned for me. Your Word in **Jeremiah 29:11**, assures me that You have good plans for my life, plans to prosper me and not to harm me, plans to give me hope and a future. I trust in Your promise, Lord, and I surrender my future into Your hands.

Guide me, O Lord, as I walk the path that You have set before me. Direct my steps and order my priorities according to Your will and not my own understanding as instructed in **Proverbs 3:5-6**. Help me to seek first Your kingdom and Your righteousness, knowing that all these things will be added unto me as mentioned in **Matthew 6:33**.

Father, I pray for wisdom and discernment as I make decisions about my future. In **James 1:5**, Your Word declares that if any of us lacks wisdom, we should ask You, who gives generously to all without finding fault, and it will be given to us. Grant me the wisdom to make choices that align with Your plans and purposes for my life.

I surrender my hopes, dreams, and ambitions to You, Lord, knowing that You are the author and perfecter of my faith as written in **Hebrews 12:2**. Help me to trust in Your timing and to wait patiently for Your guidance. May my heart be open to Your leading, and may I be obedient to Your voice as You direct my steps.

Father, I pray for protection and provision for the journey ahead. As written in **Psalm 23:1-4**, Your Word assures me that You are my shepherd, and I shall not want. You lead me beside quiet waters and restore my soul. Even though I walk through the valley of the shadow of death, I will fear no evil, for You are with me; Your rod and Your staff, they comfort me.

Thank You, Father, for the assurance of Your presence and Your provision. As I step into the future that You have prepared for me, may I walk in faith and confidence, knowing that You are always with me. May my life bring glory to Your name and be a testimony to Your goodness and faithfulness.

In Jesus' name, I pray,
Amen.

Prayer for
Generosity

Heavenly Father,

We come before You with grateful hearts, acknowledging that every good and perfect gift comes from You. As mentioned in **James 1:17, "Every good and perfect gift is from above, coming down from the Father of the heavenly lights, who does not change like shifting shadows."**

We thank You for the privilege of giving and for the example of Your sacrificial love. Your Word teaches us in **2 Corinthians 9:7, "Each of you should give what you have decided in your heart to give, not reluctantly or under compulsion, for God loves a cheerful giver."** Lord, we pray that You would cultivate within us a heart of generosity and compassion, mirroring Your own heart of abundant grace and mercy. Help us to recognize that everything we have belongs to You, and to steward our resources faithfully for Your kingdom purposes.

Grant us wisdom to discern how best to use our time, talents, and treasures to bless others and advance Your kingdom. May we give freely and joyfully, knowing that as we sow generously, we will also reap generously as we are taught in **2 Corinthians 9:6**. Teach us to give with open hands, releasing our grip on earthly possessions and trusting in Your provision. Help us to be generous not only with our material wealth, but also with our love, kindness, and compassion towards others.

Lord Jesus, You demonstrated the ultimate act of giving by laying down Your life for us on the cross. May Your sacrificial love inspire us to love and serve others selflessly, following Your example of humility and service.

Father, we pray for those who are in need. As written in **Philippians 4:19**, that You would provide for them abundantly and meet their every need according to Your riches in glory. Use us as vessels of Your grace and instruments of Your love to bring hope and healing to those who are hurting.

Help us to remember the words of Jesus in **Acts 20:35** who said, **"It is more blessed to give than to receive"**. May we experience the joy and blessing that comes from a heart that is open-handed and generous. In all our giving, may we do so with a spirit of gratitude and thanksgiving, knowing that You are the ultimate Giver and that every good gift comes from You. May our giving bring glory to Your name and advance Your kingdom here on earth.

In Jesus' name, we pray,
Amen.

Prayer for
Gentleness

Heavenly Father,

We come before You with hearts open to receive Your grace and guidance. Your Word teaches us in **Galatians 5:22-23** the importance of gentleness, and reminding us that the fruit of the Spirit includes gentleness. Help us, Lord, to cultivate this virtue in our lives.

Teach us, O God, to be gentle in our words and actions, following the example of Jesus Christ, who was gentle and humble in heart as written in **Matthew 11:29**. May our speech be seasoned with grace, bringing healing and encouragement to those we interact with. As written in **Colossians 4:6, "Let your conversation be always full of grace, seasoned with salt, so that you may know how to answer everyone."**

Father, grant us the wisdom to be gentle in our dealings with others, showing kindness and compassion to all, just as You have shown us kindness and compassion as we are taught in **Ephesians 4:32**. Help us to be patient and understanding, bearing with one another in love as written in **Ephesians 4:2**.

Lord, we recognize that gentleness is a sign of strength, not weakness. Empower us to exercise self-control and to respond to others with gentleness, even in challenging situations. As we learn in **Proverbs 15:1, "A gentle answer turns away wrath, but a harsh word stirs up anger."**

Holy Spirit, fill us with Your presence and enable us to walk in gentleness in every aspect of our lives. May our gentleness reflect Your character and draw others closer to You.

We commit ourselves to grow in gentleness, knowing that it is pleasing in Your sight and brings glory to Your name. May our lives be a testimony to the transformative power of Your Spirit working within us.

In Jesus' name, we pray,
Amen.

Prayer for
Gift of Speech

Heavenly Father,

We come before You with hearts full of gratitude for the gift of speech and communication. Your Word teaches us in **Proverbs 16:24, "Gracious words are a honeycomb, sweet to the soul and healing to the bones."** We pray that our speech may always reflect Your grace and truth, bringing healing and encouragement to those who hear.

Lord, as we prepare to speak, we ask for Your guidance and anointing upon our words. As written in **Psalm 19:14, "May these words of my mouth and this meditation of my heart be pleasing in your sight, Lord, my Rock and my Redeemer."**

Fill us with Your Holy Spirit, that our speech may be infused with wisdom, love, and compassion.

Grant us clarity of thought and eloquence of expression, that we may communicate Your truth effectively and powerfully. Help us to speak with confidence, knowing that You are with us and will give us the words to say in every situation as assured in **Luke 12:12**.

Lord Jesus, You are the Word made flesh, full of grace and truth as written in **John 1:14**. Teach us to speak with grace, seasoned with salt, so that we may know how to answer everyone as we are taught in **Colossians 4:6**. May our speech always point others to You and glorify Your holy name.

Father, we pray for humility in our speech, recognizing that our words have the power to build up or tear down as written in **Proverbs 18:21**. Help us to use our words wisely, speaking with kindness, patience, and humility.

We also lift up those who struggle with speech impediments or communication challenges. May Your grace abound in their lives, giving them confidence and courage to overcome obstacles and share Your love with others.

May our speech be a reflection of Your love and truth, bringing glory to Your name.

In Jesus' name, we pray,
Amen.

Prayer for
God's Love

Heavenly Father,

As I come before You today, I am overwhelmed by the depth of Your love for me. Your Word reminds me in **1 John 4:16** that **"God is love. Whoever lives in love lives in God, and God in them."** Thank You, Lord, for Your unfailing and unconditional love that sustains me each day.

Father, help me to always remember the magnitude of Your love. In moments of doubt or fear, may I find refuge in Your loving embrace. Your Word in **Romans 8:38-39** assures me that **"neither death nor life, neither angels nor demons, neither the present nor the future, nor any powers, neither height nor depth, nor anything else in all creation, will be able to separate us from the love of God that is in Christ Jesus our Lord."** Thank You for the security and assurance that Your love provides.

Lord, may Your love compel me to love others as You have loved me. Help me to extend grace, forgiveness, and compassion to those around me, reflecting Your love in all my interactions. Your Word in **John 13:34-35** commands us to love one another as You have loved us, so that the world may know that we are Your disciples.

Father, I pray for a deeper understanding of Your love each day. Open my eyes to see the countless ways You express Your love towards me, and may my heart overflow with gratitude and praise. Teach me to abide in Your love and to walk in obedience to Your commandments.

Thank You, Lord, for the immeasurable gift of Your love. May it be the foundation of my life and the driving force behind all that I do.

In Jesus' name, I pray,
Amen

Prayer for God's Will be done on Earth

Heavenly Father,

We come before You in humble submission, acknowledging Your sovereignty over all creation. Your Word teaches us in **Matthew 6:10, "Your kingdom come, your will be done, on earth as it is in heaven." We pray earnestly that Your divine will be manifested here on earth just as it is in heaven.** Lord, Your will is perfect, holy, and just. Your Word assures us in **Psalm 18:30, "As for God, his way is perfect: The Lord's word is flawless."** Grant us the grace to align our hearts and lives with Your will, surrendering our own desires and agendas to Your divine purpose.

Father, Your will is revealed to us through Your Word. Your commandments are righteous and true, guiding us in the paths of righteousness. Your Word declares in **Psalm 119:105, "Your word is a lamp for my feet and a light on my path." May we faithfully obey Your Word, walking in obedience and faithfulness to Your commands.** Lord Jesus, You modeled perfect obedience to the Father's will during Your earthly ministry. Your Word declares in **John 6:38, "For I have come down from heaven not to do my will but to do the will of him who sent me."** Help us to follow Your example, surrendering our will to Yours and seeking to fulfill Your purposes in our lives.

Father, Your will encompasses our salvation and redemption. Your Word declares in **1 Timothy 2:3-4, "This is good, and pleases God our Savior, who wants all people to be saved and to come to a knowledge of the truth."** May Your will for salvation be fulfilled in the hearts of all people, drawing them into a saving relationship with You through faith in Jesus Christ. Lord, Your will includes justice, mercy, and compassion for the oppressed and marginalized. Your Word commands us in **Micah 6:8, "He has shown you, O mortal, what is good. And what does the Lord require of you?** To act justly and to love mercy and to walk humbly with your God." May we actively seek to bring about Your kingdom of justice and righteousness here on earth.

Father, Your will encompasses reconciliation and unity among believers. Your Word implores us in **Ephesians 4:3, "Make every effort to keep the unity of the Spirit through the bond of peace."** May Your will for unity prevail among

Prayer for God's Will be done on Earth

Your people, transcending differences and divisions, as we are united in our love for You and one another. Lord, Your will extends to the restoration and renewal of all creation. Your Word proclaims in **Revelation 21:5, "He who was seated on the throne said, 'I am making everything new!'"** May Your will for restoration be fulfilled, bringing healing and wholeness to broken lives, relationships, and communities. Father, we surrender ourselves to Your will, trusting in Your wisdom, goodness, and faithfulness. Your Word assures us in **Romans 8:28, "And we know that in all things God works for the good of those who love Him, who have been called according to His purpose."** May Your will be done on earth as it is in heaven, for Your glory and honor forever and ever.

In Jesus' name, we pray,
Amen.

Prayer for
Good Weather

Heavenly Father,

We come before You with hearts full of gratitude for Your creation and Your sovereignty over the weather. Your Word tells us in **Psalm 147:8, "He covers the sky with clouds; he supplies the earth with rain and makes grass grow on the hills."** We acknowledge that You are in control of all things, including the weather.

Lord, we pray for good weather in accordance with Your will. We ask that You would grant us favorable conditions for our plans and activities, whether it be for outdoor events, agricultural endeavors, or simply for safe travel.

Father, You are the one who commands the winds and the waves, and they obey Your voice. We trust in Your wisdom and Your goodness to provide for our needs and to bless us with the weather that is best suited for our circumstances.

Lord, we also pray for Your protection during times of inclement weather. Your Word assures us in **Psalm 91:11-12, "For he will command his angels concerning you to guard you in all your ways; they will lift you up in their hands, so that you will not strike your foot against a stone."** May Your angels watch over us and keep us safe from harm.

Father, we commit our plans and our activities into Your hands, trusting in Your provision and Your guidance. Help us to trust in Your timing and to be content with whatever weather You send our way, knowing that You are working all things together for our good.

In Jesus' name we pray,
Amen.

Prayer for
Government and Politicians

Heavenly Father,

I lift up our government and our politicians before You, knowing that You are the ultimate authority over all nations and rulers. Your Word tells us in **1 Timothy 2:1-2, "I urge, then, first of all, that petitions, prayers, intercession and thanksgiving be made for all people, for kings and all those in authority, that we may live peaceful and quiet lives in all godliness and holiness."**

Lord, I pray for wisdom, discernment, and integrity for our government leaders and politicians. May they seek Your guidance and rely on Your principles as they make decisions that affect the welfare of our nation and its citizens.

Father, I ask that You would grant them humility and a servant's heart, putting the needs of the people above their own interests. Help them to govern with justice, fairness, and compassion, seeking the well-being of all, especially the marginalized and vulnerable in our society.

Lord, I pray for unity and cooperation among our leaders, that they may work together for the common good and set aside partisan divisions and personal agendas. Your Word reminds us in **Proverbs 11:14, "For lack of guidance a nation falls, but victory is won through many advisers."** I pray that they would seek wise counsel and be open to constructive dialogue and collaboration.

Father, I also lift up our nation to You, praying for peace, stability, and prosperity. May Your will be done on earth as it is in heaven, and may our government and politicians be instruments of Your peace and justice in the world.

Lord, we trust in Your sovereignty and Your faithfulness to guide and direct the affairs of nations. We commit our government and our politicians into Your hands, knowing that You are able to accomplish far more than we could ever ask or imagine.

In Jesus' name we pray,
Amen.

Prayer for
Grace

Heavenly Father,

We come before You with humble hearts, acknowledging Your abundant grace poured out upon us each day. Your Word declares in **Ephesians 2:8-9, "For it is by grace you have been saved, through faith and this is not from yourselves, it is the gift of God, not by works, so that no one can boast."** We are grateful for the unmerited favor and love You have shown us through Your grace.

Lord, Your grace is our foundation and our strength. It sustains us in times of trial and empowers us to walk in Your ways. Your Word teaches us in **2 Corinthians 12:9, "My grace is sufficient for you, for my power is made perfect in weakness."** Help us to rely fully on Your grace, knowing that Your strength is made perfect in our weakness.

Father, we confess that we often fall short of Your glory and fail to live according to Your will. Yet, Your grace is greater than our sins, as stated in **Romans 5:20, "But where sin increased, grace increased all the more."** We thank You for the forgiveness and redemption offered to us through the sacrifice of Your Son, Jesus Christ.

Grant us, O Lord, a deeper understanding of Your grace and its transformative power in our lives. Your Word reminds us in **Titus 2:11-12, "For the grace of God has appeared that offers salvation to all people. It teaches us to say 'No' to ungodliness and worldly passions, and to live self-controlled, upright and godly lives in this present age."** May Your grace continually mold us into the image of Christ and empower us to live holy and righteous lives.

Father, we pray for Your grace to abound in our relationships, our communities, and our world. Help us to extend grace and forgiveness to others as You have graciously forgiven us, as instructed in **Colossians 3:13, "Bear with each other and forgive one another if any of you has a grievance against someone. Forgive as the Lord forgave you."** Lord, we thank You for the promise of eternal life through Your grace, as proclaimed in **Titus 3:7, "So that, having been justified by his grace, we might become heirs having the hope of eternal life."** May we live each day in the assurance of Your grace and the hope of the glorious inheritance awaiting us in Your kingdom.

In Jesus' name, we pray,
Amen.

Prayer for
Grandma (Grandmother)

Heavenly Father,

I come before You today with a heart full of love and gratitude for my grandma, ***[Grandma's Name]***. Thank You for the gift of her presence in my life and for the love, wisdom, and guidance she has provided throughout the years. As it is written in **Proverbs 17:6, "Children's children are a crown to the aged, and parents are the pride of their children."** Lord, I pray for my grandma's health and well-being. Grant her strength, vitality, and peace in her body, mind, and spirit. Surround her with Your healing presence, and may any pain or discomfort she experiences be eased by Your loving touch. As it is written in **Psalm 103:2-3, "Praise the Lord, my soul, and forget not all his benefits—who forgives all your sins and heals all your diseases."**

Father, I also lift up my grandma's spiritual journey to You. Draw her closer to You each day, deepening her faith and trust in Your goodness and mercy. May she find comfort and strength in knowing You and experiencing Your presence in her life. As it is written in **James 4:8, "Come near to God and he will come near to you."**

Guide my grandma in her thoughts, words, and actions. Give her wisdom, discernment, and understanding, and help her to walk in integrity and righteousness. May she be a shining example of Your love and grace to those around her, reflecting Your light in all that she does. As it is written in **Matthew 5:16, "In the same way, let your light shine before others, that they may see your good deeds and glorify your Father in heaven."** Lord, I ask for Your protection over my grandma, both physically and spiritually. Guard her against harm and keep her safe from the schemes of the enemy. Surround her with Your angels and cover her with Your peace. As it is written in **Psalm 91:11-12, "For he will command his angels concerning you to guard you in all your ways; they will lift you up in their hands, so that you will not strike your foot against a stone."**

As I lift up my grandma in prayer today, I thank You for the blessing she is in my life and in the lives of others. May she feel Your presence and love surrounding her always. I commit my grandma into Your loving hands, trusting in Your faithfulness to watch over her and to guide her in all her ways.

In Jesus' name I pray,
Amen.

Prayer for Grandpa (Grandfather)

Heavenly Father,

We come before You with hearts full of gratitude for the gift of our dear grandpa, *[Grandpa's Name]*. Thank You for the love, wisdom, and guidance he has provided to our family throughout the years. We lift him up to You, knowing that You are the ultimate healer and comforter.

Lord, we pray for our Grandpa's health and well-being. Your Word says in **Psalm 41:3, "The Lord sustains them on their sickbed and restores them from their bed of illness."** We ask for Your healing touch to be upon him, restoring strength to his body and peace to his spirit.

Father, we also pray for his spiritual journey. May he continue to grow in faith and draw closer to You each day. Help him to find comfort and strength in Your presence, knowing that You are always with him, as **Psalm 23:4** assures us, **"Even though I walk through the darkest valley, I will fear no evil, for you are with me; your rod and your staff, they comfort me."**

Guide him in the paths of righteousness, and may he continue to be a shining example of Your love and grace to those around him. Your Word in **Proverbs 16:31** reminds us, **"Gray hair is a crown of splendor; it is attained in the way of righteousness."** May his life be a testimony to Your faithfulness and goodness.

Lord, we ask for Your peace to surround our Grandpa and our family during this time. Help us to trust in Your perfect plan and to lean on You for strength and comfort. Your Word assures us in **Isaiah 41:10, "So do not fear, for I am with you; do not be dismayed, for I am your God. I will strengthen you and help you; I will uphold you with my righteous right hand."**

We commit him into Your loving hands, knowing that You are the God of all comfort and the source of every good thing. May Your presence be felt tangibly in his life, bringing him peace, joy, and healing.

In Jesus' name we pray,
Amen.

Prayer for Gratitude

Heavenly Father,

I come before You today with a heart full of gratitude, knowing that every good and perfect gift comes from You as written in **James 1:17**. Your Word teaches us to give thanks in all circumstances, for this is Your will for us in Christ Jesus as mentioned in **1 Thessalonians 5:18**.

Lord, I thank You for the countless blessings You have bestowed upon me, both big and small. Thank You for the gift of life, for health and strength, for family and friends, for provision and protection. Thank You for Your unfailing love and faithfulness that never ceases, even when I am undeserving.

Father, I thank You for the gift of salvation through Your Son Jesus Christ. Thank You for the forgiveness of sins and the promise of eternal life with You. Help me to always remember the sacrifice Jesus made on the cross for my redemption and to live each day in gratitude for Your grace.

Lord, I thank You for the beauty of creation that surrounds me, for the majesty of Your handiwork displayed in the heavens and the earth. Your Word declares in **Psalm 19:1, "The heavens declare the glory of God; the skies proclaim the work of his hands."**

Father, I pray that You would cultivate a spirit of gratitude within me, even in the midst of trials and difficulties. Help me to trust in Your goodness and faithfulness, knowing that You are working all things together for my good as written in **Romans 8:28**. May my heart overflow with thanksgiving and praise to You, both now and forevermore.

In Jesus' name, I pray,
Amen.

Prayer for Grievances

Heavenly Father,

In this time of sorrow and grief, we come before You, seeking Your comfort and solace. Your word tells us in **Psalm 34:18, "The Lord is close to the brokenhearted and saves those who are crushed in spirit."** We take refuge in Your presence, knowing that You are with us in our pain.

Lord, we bring before You the burdens of our hearts, the weight of our sorrow, and the depth of our loss. You understand our grief more than anyone else, for Your Son, Jesus Christ, experienced sorrow and suffering on the cross for our sake.

Father, we ask for Your peace that surpasses all understanding to guard our hearts and minds in Christ Jesus as instructed in **Philippians 4:7**. May Your comforting presence envelop us, bringing healing to our wounded spirits and hope to our weary souls.

Lord, Your word assures us in **Psalm 30:5** that **"weeping may stay for the night, but rejoicing comes in the morning."** We cling to the hope of Your promises, trusting that You will turn our mourning into dancing and our sorrow into joy.

Father, help us to find strength and comfort in Your word, knowing that You are our refuge and strength, a very present help in trouble as written in **Psalm 46:1**. May Your Holy Spirit minister to us, bringing comfort, peace, and healing to our grieving hearts.

Lord, we surrender our pain and our sorrow into Your hands, trusting that You will work all things together for our good. Help us to lean on You in this time of need and to find rest in Your loving embrace.

Father, we thank You for Your faithfulness and Your compassion toward us. May Your grace sustain us in our grief and Your love surround us with comfort and hope.

In Jesus' name, we pray,
Amen.

Prayer for Growth

Heavenly Father,

We come before You with hearts full of gratitude for the opportunity to grow in grace and knowledge of You. Your Word teaches us in **2 Peter 3:18, "But grow in the grace and knowledge of our Lord and Savior Jesus Christ. To him be glory both now and forever! Amen."**

Lord, we desire to grow spiritually, to deepen our relationship with You, and to become more like Christ in every aspect of our lives. We acknowledge that true growth comes from You alone, and we surrender ourselves to Your transformative work in our hearts and minds.

Grant us wisdom and discernment as we study Your Word, meditate on Your teachings, and seek Your will for our lives. Help us to understand Your truth more fully and to apply it to our daily walk with You. Father, we pray for spiritual maturity, that we may be rooted and grounded in Your love, growing in faith, hope, and love as we learn in **Ephesians 3:17-19**. Strengthen us in our inner being by Your Spirit, that Christ may dwell in our hearts through faith as written in **Ephesians 3:16-17**.

Lord, we also pray for growth in character, that we may bear the fruit of the Spirit: love, joy, peace, patience, kindness, goodness, faithfulness, gentleness, and self-control as written in **Galatians 5:22-23**. Mold us and shape us into vessels of honor, fit for Your use and Your glory.

Father, we lift up our relationships, our careers, our ministries, and every area of our lives to You. As we are taught in **Colossians 4:5-6**, may we grow in wisdom and understanding, making the most of every opportunity to glorify You and to serve others in love.

Lord Jesus, You are the vine, and we are the branches. Apart from You, we can do nothing. Help us to **abide in** You, to remain connected to You, drawing **strength and** nourishment from Your Word and Your Spirit.

May our lives be a reflection of Your grace and **goodness,** shining brightly as lights in this world as You have **taught us** in **Matthew 5:16.** And may all the glory and honor be unto You, both now and forevermore.

In Jesus' name, we pray,
Amen.

Prayer for
Happiness

Heavenly Father,

We come before You today with hearts filled with gratitude for the gift of happiness that You provide. Your Word reminds us in **Psalm 144:15, "blessed is the people whose God is the Lord."** We thank You for being our source of joy and happiness, regardless of our circumstances.

Lord, we pray that You would fill our hearts with Your joy and peace, as **Romans 15:13** says, **"May the God of hope fill you with all joy and peace as you trust in him, so that you may overflow with hope by the power of the Holy Spirit."** Help us to find true happiness in You alone, knowing that Your love for us is everlasting and unchanging.

Guide us, O Lord, to delight in Your ways, as **Psalm 37:4** encourages us, **"Take delight in the Lord, and he will give you the desires of your heart."** May our greatest joy come from knowing You and following Your will for our lives.

Father, we ask for Your grace to overcome any obstacles or challenges that may hinder our happiness. Your Word assures us in **Philippians 4:6-7, "Do not be anxious about anything, but in every situation, by prayer and petition, with thanksgiving, present your requests to God. And the peace of God, which transcends all understanding, will guard your hearts and your minds in Christ Jesus."** Grant us the peace that surpasses all understanding, and help us to trust in Your perfect plan for our lives.

Teach us to find joy in serving others, as Jesus Himself taught us in **Mark 10:45, "For even the Son of Man did not come to be served, but to serve, and to give his life as a ransom for many."** May we experience true happiness as we follow Your example of selfless love and service to others.

Lord, we commit our pursuit of happiness into Your hands, knowing that true and lasting joy can only be found in You. Help us to seek You above all else and to trust in Your promises, knowing that You are faithful to fulfill them.

In Jesus' name, we pray,
Amen.

Prayer for Healing

Heavenly Father,

We come before You with hearts full of faith, believing in Your power to heal and restore. We lift up **[Name]**, who is in need of Your healing touch. As it is written in **James 5:15, "And the prayer offered in faith will make the sick person well; the Lord will raise them up. If they have sinned, they will be forgiven."**

Lord Jesus, You are the Great Physician, You are the Great doctor, and by Your wounds, we are healed. We ask that You would lay Your hands upon **[Name]** and bring healing to every area of **his/her** body, mind, and spirit that is in need. As it is written in **Isaiah 53:5, "But he was pierced for our transgressions, he was crushed for our iniquities; the punishment that brought us peace was on him, and by his wounds, we are healed."**

We rebuke any sickness, disease, or pain that is afflicting **[Name]**, and we declare Your promise of healing over their life. Let Your healing power flow through them, restore them, renew every cell and every organ. May You do a dialysis in their body by Your blood.

We also pray for strength and comfort for **[Name]** during this time of illness.

Surround **her/him** with Your peace that surpasses all understanding and fill them with hope and courage to face each day with faith. As it is written in **Philippians 4:7, "And the peace of God, which transcends all understanding, will guard your hearts and your minds in Christ Jesus."**

Lord, we know that Your ways are higher than our ways, and Your thoughts are higher than our thoughts. Even in the midst of suffering, we trust in Your goodness and Your plan for **[Name]**'s life.

May this experience of healing be a testimony to Your grace and mercy, and may **[Name]**'s life be a living testimony to Your healing power.

In Jesus' name we pray,
Amen.

Prayer for Health

Heavenly Father,

We come before You today, acknowledging that You are the Great Physician, the one who heals all our diseases as written in **Psalm 103:3**. We thank You for the gift of health and wellness, recognizing that every good and perfect gift comes from You. It is said in **James 1:17, "Every good and perfect gift is from above, coming down from the Father of the heavenly lights, who does not change like shifting shadows."**

Lord, we lift up our bodies, minds, and spirits to You, asking for Your healing touch to be upon us. Your word in **Isaiah 53:5**, tells us that by Your stripes, we are healed, so we claim that promise over our lives today.

We pray for physical healing, Lord. Heal any sickness, disease, or infirmity that may be afflicting us. Restore our bodies to full health and vitality and strengthen us with Your power and might.

We also pray for emotional and mental health, Lord. Bring peace to our minds and hearts, casting out all anxiety, fear, and depression. Fill us with Your joy and hope, knowing that You are always with us and that we can trust in Your unfailing love.

And we pray for spiritual health, Lord. Draw us closer to You each day, deepening our faith and trust in Your goodness and mercy. Help us to walk in obedience to Your word and to live lives that honor and glorify You.

We surrender our health into Your hands, knowing that You are able to do immeasurably more than all we ask or imagine as mentioned in **Ephesians 3:20**. May Your will be done in our lives, and may we experience the fullness of Your healing power.

In Jesus' name we pray,
Amen.

Prayer for
Heart for Missions

Heavenly Father,

I come before You with a heart that is burdened for missions, knowing that Your Word in **Matthew 28:19** instructs us to go and make disciples of all nations. You have called us to be Your witnesses, both near and far, proclaiming the good news of Jesus Christ to all people as written in **Acts 1:8**.

Lord, I pray that You would ignite within me a passion for missions, a burning desire to see Your name glorified among the nations. Give me eyes to see the lost and the hurting, and a heart that breaks for what breaks Yours. As written in **Psalm 34:18, "The Lord is close to the brokenhearted and saves those who are crushed in spirit."**

Father, I thank You for the example of missionaries throughout history who have sacrificially laid down their lives to spread the gospel. May their dedication and perseverance inspire me to wholeheartedly commit myself to the task of reaching the unreached with the message of salvation.

Lord, I pray for the unreached people groups around the world, those who have never heard the name of Jesus. May Your Spirit move in their hearts, drawing them to Yourself and opening their eyes to the truth of Your love and grace.

Father, I ask for divine appointments and opportunities to share the gospel wherever I go, whether it be in my own community or in distant lands. Help me to be bold and courageous in proclaiming the name of Jesus, knowing that You are with me always, to the very end of the age as assured in **Matthew 28:20**.

Lord, I commit myself to Your mission, surrendering my will and my plans to Yours. Use me as a vessel of Your love and grace, that others may come to know the saving power of Jesus Christ and experience the joy of salvation.

In Jesus' name, I pray,
Amen.

Prayer for Heaven

Heavenly Father,

We come before You with hearts full of gratitude and awe, acknowledging Your sovereignty over all things, including heaven and earth. Your Word assures us in **Psalm 115:16, "The highest heavens belong to the Lord, but the earth he has given to mankind."**

Lord, we thank You for the promise of heaven, a place of eternal joy, peace, and communion with You. Your Word declares in **Revelation 21:4, "He will wipe every tear from their eyes. There will be no more death or mourning or crying or pain, for the old order of things has passed away."**

We long for the day when we will dwell in Your presence forever, experiencing the fullness of Your glory and love. As Jesus promised in **John 14:2-3, "My Father's house has many rooms; if that were not so, would I have told you that I am going there to prepare a place for you? And if I go and prepare a place for you, I will come back and take you to be with me that you also may be where I am."**

Lord, help us to fix our eyes on the hope of heaven, especially in times of trial and uncertainty. Give us the assurance that this world is not our final home, but that we are citizens of heaven, eagerly awaiting the return of our Savior, Jesus Christ as clearly written in **Philippians 3:20-21**.

May the reality of heaven inspire us to live with purpose and eternity in mind, seeking first Your kingdom and Your righteousness as we are taught in **Matthew 6:33**. Help us to store up treasures in heaven, where moth and rust do not destroy and where thieves do not break in and steal as written in **Matthew 6:20**.

Lord, we pray for those who have not yet accepted Your gift of salvation and the hope of heaven. May Your Spirit convict their hearts and lead them to repentance and faith in Jesus Christ, so that they too may inherit eternal life as promised in **John 3:16**.

As we await the fulfillment of Your promise of heaven, may we live each day in anticipation and readiness for the glorious day when we will be united with You in heaven forever.

In Jesus' name, we pray,
Amen.

Prayer for Holy Communion

Heavenly Father,

As we gather around Your table to partake in the holy communion, we come before You with reverence and gratitude for the sacrifice of Your Son, Jesus Christ, who gave His body and blood for our redemption. Your Word instructs us in **1 Corinthians 11:23-26, "For I received from the Lord what I also passed on to you: The Lord Jesus, on the night he was betrayed, took bread, and when he had given thanks, he broke it and said, "This is my body, which is for you; do this in remembrance of me." In the same way, after supper he took the cup, saying, "This cup is the new covenant in my blood; do this, whenever you drink it, in remembrance of me." For whenever you eat this bread and drink this cup, you proclaim the Lord's death until he comes."**

Father, as we partake of the bread and the cup, symbols of Christ's broken body and shed blood, we remember the depth of Your love for us and the price Jesus paid for our salvation. We thank You for the forgiveness of sins and the reconciliation we have with You through His sacrifice. We come before You with hearts of repentance, confessing our sins and asking for Your forgiveness. Your Word assures us in **1 John 1:9, "If we confess our sins, he is faithful and just and will forgive us our sins and purify us from all unrighteousness."** Cleanse us, O Lord, and renew us by the power of Your Spirit as we partake in this holy sacrament.

May this communion strengthen our union with Christ and with one another as members of His body, the church. Your Word teaches us in **1 Corinthians 10:16-17: "Is not the cup of thanksgiving for which we give thanks a participation in the blood of Christ? And is not the bread that we break a participation in the body of Christ? Because there is one loaf, we, who are many, are one body, for we all share the one loaf."**

Help us to discern the body of Christ and to live in unity and love with our brothers and sisters in Christ. May this communion deepen our faith, nourish our souls, and empower us to live lives that honor and glorify You.

We give You thanks, Lord, for the privilege of partaking in this sacred meal and for the assurance of Your presence with us. May our lives be a living testimony to the reality of Christ's death and resurrection until He comes again.

In Jesus' name, we pray,
Amen.

Prayer for Holy Spirit

Heavenly Father,

We come before You in reverence and awe, acknowledging the power and presence of Your Holy Spirit in our lives. Your word teaches us in **Acts 1:8, "But you will receive power when the Holy Spirit comes on you; and you will be my witnesses in Jerusalem, and in all Judea and Samaria, and to the ends of the earth."**

Lord, we thank You for the gift of Your Holy Spirit, who dwells within us, guiding, empowering, and transforming us into the image of Christ. Your Spirit is our Comforter, our Counselor, and our Advocate, leading us into all truth and righteousness.

Father, we pray for a fresh outpouring of Your Holy Spirit upon us today. Fill us anew with Your Spirit, saturating every aspect of our being with Your presence and power. Your word assures us in **Luke 11:13, "If you then, though you are evil, know how to give good gifts to your children, how much more will your Father in heaven give the Holy Spirit to those who ask him!"**

Lord, we surrender ourselves fully to the leading of Your Holy Spirit. Grant us ears to hear Your voice, hearts to obey Your promptings, and feet to walk in Your ways. Help us to yield to Your Spirit's guidance in every decision, every action, and every thought. Father, Your Spirit equips us with spiritual gifts for the edification of the body of Christ and for the advancement of Your kingdom.

We pray for a greater manifestation of the gifts of the Spirit in our lives, according to **1 Corinthians 12:7-11** which says, **"Now to each one the manifestation of the Spirit is given for the common good. To one there is given through the Spirit a message of wisdom, to another a message of knowledge by means of the same Spirit, to another faith by the same Spirit, to another gifts of healing by that one Spirit, to another miraculous powers, to another prophecy, to another distinguishing between spirits, to another speaking in different kinds of tongues, and to still another the interpretation of tongues. All these are the work of one and the same Spirit, and he distributes them to each one, just as he determines."**

Prayer for
Holy Spirit

Lord, as we yield to Your Spirit's work within us, may we bear the fruit of the Spirit in abundance: love, joy, peace, patience, kindness, goodness, faithfulness, gentleness, and self-control as written in **Galatians 5:22-23**.

May our lives be a living testimony to Your transforming power and grace. Father, we thank You for the promise of Your Holy Spirit, who empowers us to live victoriously and to be effective witnesses for Christ in the world. May we be filled afresh with Your Spirit each day, walking in step with You and glorifying Your holy name.

In Jesus' name, we pray,
Amen.

Prayer for Home

Heavenly Father,

We come before You with grateful hearts for the gift of our home, recognizing that it is a blessing from Your hand. Your Word reminds us in **Psalm 127:1, "Unless the Lord builds the house, the builders labor in vain. Unless the Lord watches over the city, the guards stand watch in vain."** We acknowledge that our home belongs to You, and we invite Your presence to dwell within its walls.

Lord, we pray that our home would be a place of refuge and peace, where Your love and grace abound. May Your Spirit fill every room, bringing unity, joy, and harmony among all who dwell here. Help us to cultivate an atmosphere of love and forgiveness, following the example of Christ's sacrificial love for us as shown in **Ephesians 5:2**.

Father, we ask for Your protection over our home, both physically and spiritually. Guard us against harm and evil influences and shield us from the attacks of the enemy. Your Word assures us in **Psalm 91:9-11, "If you say, "The Lord is my refuge," and you make the Most High your dwelling, no harm will overtake you, no disaster will come near your tent. For he will command his angels concerning you to guard you in all your ways"**.

Lord, we pray for wisdom and discernment as we make decisions regarding our home and family life. Help us to prioritize Your kingdom and seek Your will in all that we do.

Your Word instructs us in **Proverbs 24:3-4, "By wisdom a house is built, and through understanding it is established; through knowledge its rooms are filled with rare and beautiful treasures."** Grant us wisdom to build our home upon the foundation of Your truth and righteousness.

Father, we lift up our family members and loved ones who share this home with us. May our relationships be characterized by love, respect, and mutual support. Help us to bear one another's burdens and to encourage one another in faith.

Your Word teaches us in **Galatians 6:2, "Carry each other's burdens, and in this way, you will fulfill the law of Christ."** May our home be a place where Your love is tangibly experienced, and where hearts are drawn closer to You.

Prayer for Home

Lord, we commit our home into Your loving hands, trusting in Your provision and guidance. May it be a place where Your name is honored and glorified, and where Your presence is felt by all who enter. Use our home as a beacon of Your light and love in the world, shining brightly for Your kingdom purposes.

In Jesus' name, we pray,
Amen.

Prayer for Homeless

Heavenly Father,

We come before You with heavy hearts, deeply grieved by the plight of those who find themselves without shelter, wandering the streets, and experiencing the harsh reality of homelessness. Your Word reminds us in **Matthew 25:35-36, "For I was hungry and you gave me something to eat, I was thirsty and you gave me something to drink, I was a stranger and you invited me in, I needed clothes and you clothed me, I was sick and you looked after me, I was in prison and you came to visit me."** We pray earnestly for Your compassion and mercy to be poured out upon the homeless and for tangible solutions to end their suffering.

Lord Jesus, You, who had no place to lay Your head during Your earthly ministry, understand intimately the struggles of the homeless. Your Word teaches us in **Psalm 10:17-18, "You, Lord, hear the desire of the afflicted; you encourage them, and you listen to their cry, defending the fatherless and the oppressed, so that mere earthly mortals will never again strike terror."** We pray for Your divine intervention to provide shelter, safety, and dignity to those who are homeless.

Father, we lift up to You the organizations, shelters, and ministries that work tirelessly to provide assistance and support to the homeless. Your Word instructs us in **Isaiah 58:7, "Is it not to share your food with the hungry and to provide the poor wanderer with shelter—when you see the naked, to clothe them, and not to turn away from your own flesh and blood?"** Bless their efforts, multiply their resources, and grant them wisdom and compassion as they serve the homeless community.

Lord, we pray for governments, policymakers, and community leaders to enact policies and initiatives that address the root causes of homelessness and provide sustainable solutions. Your Word reminds us in **Proverbs 31:8-9, "Speak up for those who cannot speak for themselves, for the rights of all who are destitute. Speak up and judge fairly; defend the rights of the poor and needy."** May justice and righteousness prevail in our societies, ensuring that every person has access to safe and affordable housing.

Father, we lift up to You the individuals who are experiencing homelessness, each one known and loved by You. Your Word assures us in **Psalm 34:17-18, "The righteous cry**

Prayer for Homeless

out, and the Lord hears them; he delivers them from all their troubles. The Lord is close to the brokenhearted and saves those who are crushed in spirit."** Comfort them in their distress, provide for their needs, and guide them to the support and resources they require to rebuild their lives.

Lord, we pray for a transformation of hearts and minds within our communities, that we may extend compassion, hospitality, and support to those who are homeless. Your Word teaches us in **Hebrews 13:2, "Do not forget to show hospitality to strangers, for by so doing some people have shown hospitality to angels without knowing it."** May we see the face of Christ in the marginalized and treat them with the dignity and respect they deserve as Your beloved children.

Father, we commit the cause of ending homelessness into Your hands, trusting in Your promise to hear the cries of the afflicted and to bring justice to the oppressed. Your Word assures us in **Psalm 9:9, "The Lord is a refuge for the oppressed, a stronghold in times of trouble."** May Your kingdom of justice and mercy come, where all find refuge and belonging in Your love.

In Jesus' name, we pray,
Amen.

Prayer for
Honesty and Integrity

Heavenly Father,

I come before You with a heart that longs to walk in honesty and integrity, aligning my actions with Your righteous standards. Your Word teaches me in **Proverbs 11:3** that the integrity of the upright guides them, but the crookedness of the treacherous destroys them. Lord, I desire to be guided by integrity in all that I do, both in my words and my deeds.

Father, forgive me for the times when I have fallen short of Your standards of honesty and truthfulness. Help me to be honest in my dealings with others, speaking the truth in love, as **Ephesians 4:25** instructs. May my words be filled with integrity and my actions be characterized by honesty, reflecting the righteousness of Your character.

Grant me the strength to resist the temptation to deceive or manipulate for personal gain. Help me to walk in integrity even when faced with difficult circumstances or pressures from the world. Your Word assures me in **Psalm 25:21** that integrity and uprightness preserve me, for I wait for You.

Lord, I pray that You would cultivate within me a heart that values honesty and integrity above all else. May I be known as a person of integrity, whose words can be trusted and whose actions are consistent with Your truth. Teach me to walk in the fear of the Lord, for **Proverbs 10:9** tells me that whoever walks in integrity walks securely, but whoever takes crooked paths will be found out.

Thank You, Lord, for the example of Jesus Christ, who lived a life of perfect integrity and truthfulness. May I follow in His footsteps, imitating His character and reflecting His light to the world around me.

In Jesus' name, I pray,
Amen.

Prayer for
Hope and Courage

Heavenly Father,

I come before You in need of hope and courage, trusting in Your promises and seeking strength for the journey ahead. Your Word reminds us in **Romans 15:13, "May the God of hope fill you with all joy and peace as you trust in him, so that you may overflow with hope by the power of the Holy Spirit."**

Lord, I pray that You would infuse my heart with hope, even in the midst of challenges and uncertainties. Help me to anchor my trust in You, knowing that You are the source of all hope and that You hold my future securely in Your hands. May Your presence bring me joy and peace, filling me with confidence and assurance as I navigate the storms of life.

Grant me courage, O Lord, to face whatever lies ahead with boldness and determination. Your Word in **Joshua 1:9** encourages us, **"Have I not commanded you? Be strong and courageous. Do not be afraid; do not be discouraged, for the Lord your God will be with you wherever you go."** May I take heart in the knowledge of Your constant presence with me, knowing that You go before me and empower me to overcome every obstacle.

Help me to fix my eyes on Jesus, the author and perfecter of my faith, drawing strength from his example and his promises. Your Word in **Hebrews 10:23** assures us, **"Let us hold unswervingly to the hope we profess, for he who promised is faithful."** May I cling to the hope of Your faithfulness, knowing that You are true to Your word and that You will never leave nor forsake me.

Fill me, O Lord, with Your Holy Spirit, empowering me to live with hope and courage each day. May my life be a testimony to Your goodness and grace, shining brightly in a world that desperately needs Your light.

In Jesus' name, I pray,
Amen.

Prayer for Human Trafficking

Heavenly Father,

We come before You with heavy hearts, burdened by the pervasive evil of human trafficking that plagues our world. Your Word teaches us in **Psalm 10:18, "defending the fatherless and the oppressed, so that mere earthly mortals will never again strike terror."** Lord, we cry out to You on behalf of those who are trafficked and exploited, especially the vulnerable women, children, and men who are ensnared in this heinous crime.

Father, we acknowledge that human trafficking is a gross violation of Your commandments to love our neighbors as ourselves. Your Word admonishes us in **Proverbs 31:8-9, "Speak up for those who cannot speak for themselves, for the rights of all who are destitute. Speak up and judge fairly; defend the rights of the poor and needy."** Give us the courage to speak out against this injustice and to advocate for the rights and dignity of those who are trafficked.

Lord Jesus, You came to proclaim freedom for the captives and to bind up the brokenhearted as written in **Isaiah 61:1**. We pray for Your intervention and deliverance for those who are trapped in the chains of human trafficking. Your Word assures us in **Psalm 91:14-15, "Because he loves me," says the Lord, "I will rescue him; I will protect him, for he acknowledges my name. He will call on me, and I will answer him; I will be with him in trouble, I will deliver him and honor him."** May Your mighty hand rescue and protect them from harm.

Father, we lift up to You the perpetrators of human trafficking, those who exploit and oppress others for their own gain. Your Word warns us in **Proverbs 6:16-19, "There are six things the Lord hates, seven that are detestable to him: haughty eyes, a lying tongue, hands that shed innocent blood, a heart that devises wicked schemes, feet that are quick to rush into evil, a false witness who pours out lies and a person who stirs up conflict in the community."**

Bring conviction to their hearts, lead them to repentance, and bring them to justice for their crimes. Lord, we pray for the victims of human trafficking, many of whom endure unspeakable suffering and trauma. Your Word promises in **Isaiah 42:3, "A bruised reed he will not break, and a smoldering wick he will not snuff out. In faithfulness he will bring forth justice."** Comfort them in their pain, heal their wounds, and restore to them the dignity and worth that is theirs as Your beloved children.

Prayer for Human Trafficking

Father, we pray for those who work tirelessly to combat human trafficking, including law enforcement officers, advocates, and organizations dedicated to prevention, rescue, and restoration. Your Word encourages us in **Galatians 6:9, "Let us not become weary in doing good, for at the proper time we will reap a harvest if we do not give up."** Strengthen them in their efforts, grant them wisdom and discernment, and equip them with the resources needed to bring about lasting change.

Lord, we ask for Your Church to rise up as a powerful force against human trafficking, shining Your light into the darkness and offering hope and healing to the victims. Your Word in **Psalm 82:4**, calls us to **"rescue the weak and the needy; deliver them from the hand of the wicked"**. May Your people be bold in their advocacy, compassionate in their care, and unwavering in their commitment to justice.

Father, we commit the fight against human trafficking into Your hands, knowing that You are a God of justice and mercy. Your Word assures us in **Psalm 146:7-9, "He upholds the cause of the oppressed and gives food to the hungry. The Lord sets prisoners free, the Lord gives sight to the blind, the Lord lifts up those who are bowed down, the Lord loves the righteous. The Lord watches over the foreigner and sustains the fatherless and the widow, but he frustrates the ways of the wicked."** May Your kingdom of justice and righteousness be established on earth as it is in heaven.

In Jesus' name, we pray,
Amen.

Prayer for
Humility or Staying Humble

Heavenly Father,

I come before You humbly, recognizing that You are the source of all wisdom, strength, and grace. Your Word in **James 4:10** reminds us, **"Humble yourselves before the Lord, and he will lift you up."** Lord, I desire to cultivate humility in my heart, knowing that it is pleasing to You and essential for walking in obedience to Your will.

Forgive me, Lord, for the times when pride has crept into my thoughts and actions. Help me to follow the example of Jesus Christ, who humbled himself to the point of death on the cross. Your Word in **Philippians 2:3-4** instructs us, **"Do nothing out of selfish ambition or vain conceit. Rather, in humility value others above yourselves, not looking to your own interests but each of you to the interests of the others."** May I learn to value others above myself and to serve them with humility and love.

Lord, I surrender my will to Yours and acknowledge that apart from You, I can do nothing. Your Word in **Proverbs 11:2** reminds us, **"When pride comes, then comes disgrace, but with humility comes wisdom."** Grant me the wisdom to walk humbly before You and to seek Your guidance in all things.

Help me to recognize my dependence on You for every breath I take and every step I make. May my life be a reflection of Your love, mercy, and grace, rather than seeking recognition or praise for myself. Your Word in **Micah 6:8** instructs us, **"He has shown you, O mortal, what is good. And what does the Lord require of you? To act justly and to love mercy and to walk humbly with your God."** May I walk humbly with You, Lord, acknowledging Your sovereignty and trusting in Your plan for my life.

I pray for a humble heart that is quick to confess sin, eager to serve others, and open to correction and guidance from Your Spirit. Help me to embrace humility as a virtue to be cherished and cultivated, rather than avoided or despised.

Thank You, Lord, for Your example of humility and for the promise that You will exalt the humble. May I continually seek to humble myself before You, knowing that in Your presence, there is fullness of joy and abundant grace.

In Jesus' name, I pray,
Amen.

Prayer for Hunger

Heavenly Father,

We come before You with heavy hearts, deeply grieved by the widespread hunger and malnutrition that afflict millions of Your children around the world. Your Word teaches us in **Isaiah 58:10, "and if you spend yourselves in behalf of the hungry and satisfy the needs of the oppressed, then your light will rise in the darkness, and your night will become like the noonday."** We pray earnestly for an end to hunger and for Your light to shine brightly in the darkest corners of our world. Lord, You are the provider of all good things, and Your heart breaks for those who go without food. Your Word reminds us in **Matthew 25:35, "For I was hungry, and you gave me something to eat, I was thirsty, and you gave me something to drink, I was a stranger and you invited me in."** We ask for Your miraculous provision to feed the hungry and for Your people to be instruments of Your love and compassion in sharing their resources with those in need.

Father, we pray for wisdom and discernment for leaders and policymakers as they address the systemic issues that contribute to hunger and food insecurity. Your Word instructs us in **Proverbs 31:8-9, "Speak up for those who cannot speak for themselves, for the rights of all who are destitute. Speak up and judge fairly; defend the rights of the poor and needy."** May they enact policies and initiatives that ensure equitable access to nutritious food for all people. Lord, we lift up to You the organizations and individuals who are on the front lines of the fight against hunger, tirelessly working to provide food assistance, agricultural support, and sustainable solutions to hunger. Your Word encourages us in **Galatians 6:9, "Let us not become weary in doing good, for at the proper time we will reap a harvest if we do not give up."** Strengthen their efforts, multiply their resources, and grant them wisdom and perseverance in their mission to end hunger. Father, we pray for a transformation of hearts and minds, both in the privileged and the underprivileged, that we may see one another through Your eyes and extend compassion and generosity to those who are hungry. Your Word teaches us in **Proverbs 22:9, "The generous will themselves be blessed, for they share their food with the poor."** May we be faithful stewards of the resources You have entrusted to us, sharing generously with those in need.

Lord, we commit the cause of ending hunger into Your hands, knowing that You are a God of abundance and compassion. Your Word assures us in **Psalm 145:15-16, "The eyes of all look to you, and you give them their food at the proper time. You open your hand and satisfy the desires of every living thing."** May Your kingdom of plenty and provision come, where all hunger is satisfied and every need is met according to Your riches in glory.

In Jesus' name, we pray,
Amen.

Prayer for
Husband

Heavenly Father,

I come before You today with a heart full of gratitude for the precious gift of my husband. Your word tells us in **Proverbs 18:22, "He who finds a wife finds what is good and receives favor from the Lord."** Thank You for blessing me with his presence in my life. Lord, I lift up my husband to You, knowing that he is fearfully and wonderfully made in Your image. I thank You for his love, his strength, and his unwavering support. Your word reminds us in **Ephesians 5:25, "Husbands, love your wives, just as Christ loved the church and gave himself up for her."** Help him to love me sacrificially, just as Christ loves the church.

Father, I pray for my husband's health and well-being. Grant him physical strength, emotional peace, and spiritual vitality. Your word assures us in **Psalm 103:2-3, "Praise the Lord, my soul, and forget not all his benefits—who forgives all your sins and heals all your diseases."** May Your healing touch be upon him, restoring him to fullness of health.

Lord, I pray for my husband's spiritual journey. Draw him closer to You each day, deepening his faith and trust in Your goodness and mercy. Your word tells us in **Psalm 23:3, "He refreshes my soul. He guides me along the right paths for his name's sake."** Guide him in the paths of righteousness, and may he find refreshment and renewal in Your presence.

Father, I ask for Your protection over my husband, both physically and spiritually. Guard him against harm and keep him safe from the attacks of the enemy. Your word assures us in **Psalm 91:11-12, "For he will command his angels concerning you to guard you in all your ways; they will lift you up in their hands, so that you will not strike your foot against a stone."** Surround him with Your angels and cover him with Your peace. Lord, I thank You for the blessing my husband is in my life and in the lives of others. Help me to cherish him, honor him, and support him in all things. Your word reminds us in **Proverbs 31:10, "A wife of noble character who can find? She is worth far more than rubies."** May I always recognize and appreciate the incredible gift that he is.

I commit my husband into Your loving hands, trusting in Your faithfulness to watch over him and to guide him in all his ways.

In Jesus' name I pray,
Amen.

Prayer for
Ideas

Heavenly Father,

We come before You in humility and gratitude, acknowledging that You are the source of all wisdom, knowledge, and creativity. Your Word teaches us in **James 1:17, "Every good and perfect gift is from above, coming down from the Father of the heavenly lights, who does not change like shifting shadows."** We thank You for the gift of ideas and inspiration that You graciously bestow upon us.

Lord, we ask for Your divine guidance and inspiration as we seek ideas for various aspects of our lives. Your Word assures us in **Proverbs 16:3, "Commit to the Lord whatever you do, and he will establish your plans."** We commit our desires and aspirations to You, Lord, trusting that You will direct our steps and inspire us with Your perfect wisdom.

Father, we pray for ideas in our personal lives, careers, ministries, and relationships. Your Word encourages us in **Psalm 32:8, "I will instruct you and teach you in the way you should go; I will counsel you with my loving eye on you."** Guide us, Lord, and inspire us with ideas that align with Your will and lead us on paths of righteousness.

Lord Jesus, we ask for creative ideas in solving problems, overcoming obstacles, and seizing opportunities. Your Word declares in **Philippians 4:13, "I can do all this through him who gives me strength."** Strengthen us, Lord, and empower us with Your Spirit to think innovatively and approach every situation with faith and confidence.

Father, we pray for ideas in serving others and making a positive impact in our communities. Your Word instructs us in **Galatians 5:13, "You, my brothers and sisters, were called to be free. But do not use your freedom to indulge the flesh; rather, serve one another humbly in love."** Inspire us, Lord, to be vessels of Your love and grace, sharing Your compassion with those in need.

Lord, we commit our minds and hearts to You, trusting that You will give us the wisdom and creativity we need. Your Word promises in **Isaiah 41:10, "So do not fear, for I am with you; do not be dismayed, for I am your God. I will strengthen you and help you; I will uphold you with my righteous right hand."**

Thank You, Lord, for Your faithfulness and provision.

In Jesus' name, we pray,
Amen.

Prayer for Inspiration

Heavenly Father,

We come before You, the Creator of all things, with hearts open to receive divine ideas and inspiration from Your Holy Spirit. Your Word teaches us in **James 1:5, "If any of you lacks wisdom, you should ask God, who gives generously to all without finding fault, and it will be given to you."** We humbly ask for Your wisdom and insight, Lord, as we seek divine inspiration for every aspect of our lives. Father, we acknowledge that You are the source of all creativity and innovation. Your Word declares in **Genesis 1:1, "In the beginning God created the heavens and the earth."** Just as You spoke creation into existence, we pray that You would speak fresh ideas and inspiration into our hearts and minds. Illuminate our understanding, Lord, and reveal Your plans and purposes to us.

Lord, we ask for divine wisdom and insight in our personal lives, careers, ministries, and every area where we need direction. Your Word assures us in **Proverbs 3:5-6, "Trust in the Lord with all your heart and lean not on your own understanding; in all your ways submit to him, and he will make your paths straight."** Guide us, Lord, and lead us in the paths of righteousness for Your name's sake. Father, we pray for divine inspiration in solving problems, overcoming challenges, and finding creative solutions to difficult situations. Your Word encourages us in **Philippians 4:13, "I can do all things through him who gives me strength."** Strengthen us, Lord, and empower us with Your Spirit to think outside the box and approach every situation with faith and creativity.

Lord Jesus, we ask for divine inspiration in our relationships, that we may love others with Your love and demonstrate Your grace and compassion. Your Word instructs us in **John 13:34-35, "A new command I give you: Love one another. As I have loved you, so you must love one another. By this everyone will know that you are my disciples, if you love one another."** Fill us with Your love, Lord, and inspire us to love others sacrificially. Father, we pray for divine inspiration in sharing Your Gospel and making disciples of all nations. Your Word commands us in **Matthew 28:19-20, "Therefore go and make disciples of all nations, baptizing them in the name of the Father and of the Son and of the Holy Spirit, and teaching them to obey everything I have commanded you. And surely I am with you always, to the very end of the age."** Equip us, Lord, with boldness and clarity as we share the good news of salvation through Jesus Christ.

Lord, we commit our hearts and minds to You, trusting in Your promise to give wisdom to those who ask. May Your Holy Spirit guide us into all truth and inspire us to live lives that bring glory and honor to Your name.

In Jesus' name, we pray,
Amen.

Prayer for Jealousy

Heavenly Father,

We come before You with hearts burdened by the sin of jealousy. Your Word teaches us in **James 3:16** that **"For where you have envy and selfish ambition, there you find disorder and every evil practice."** We acknowledge that jealousy is a destructive force that leads to strife, division, and broken relationships. We humbly confess our struggles with jealousy and ask for Your forgiveness and transformation.

Lord, we recognize that jealousy stems from insecurity, comparison, and covetousness. Your Word warns us against the dangers of jealousy in **Proverbs 14:30, "A heart at peace gives life to the body, but envy rots the bones."** We acknowledge that jealousy corrodes our souls and damages our relationships. Forgive us for allowing jealousy to take root in our hearts and minds. Father, we pray for Your Spirit to work in us, transforming our hearts and renewing our minds. Your Word tells us in **Romans 12:2, "Do not conform to the pattern of this world, but be transformed by the renewing of your mind. Then you will be able to test and approve what God's will is—his good, pleasing and perfect will."** Help us to reject the lies of jealousy and to embrace the truth of Your love and provision for us.

Lord, we ask for Your grace to replace our jealousy with gratitude and contentment. Your Word reminds us in **Hebrews 13:5, "Keep your lives free from the love of money and be content with what you have, because God has said, "Never will I leave you; never will I forsake you.""** Help us to trust in Your promises and to find our satisfaction in You alone. Father, we pray for the strength to celebrate the success and blessings of others without feeling threatened or envious. Your Word instructs us in **Romans 12:15** to **"Rejoice with those who rejoice; mourn with those who mourn."** May we genuinely rejoice with others in their victories and blessings, knowing that You are the giver of every good gift.

Lord, we ask for Your help to guard our hearts against the destructive influence of jealousy. Your Word encourages us in **Philippians 4:6-7, "Do not be anxious about anything, but in every situation, by prayer and petition, with thanksgiving, present your requests to God. And the peace of God, which transcends all understanding, will guard your hearts and your minds in Christ Jesus."** Grant us Your peace that surpasses all understanding and guard our hearts with Your love.

Father, we surrender our struggles with jealousy into Your hands and ask for Your strength to overcome. Help us to walk in humility, gratitude, and love, reflecting Your character to the world around us.

In Jesus' name, we pray,
Amen.

Prayer for Job Interview

Heavenly Father,

I come before You today with a heart full of gratitude for the opportunity to seek employment, knowing that You are the provider of all good things as promised in **James 1:17**. I acknowledge that every opportunity I receive is a gift from You, and I trust in Your guidance and provision.

Lord, Your Word assures us in **Philippians 4:6-7, "Do not be anxious about anything, but in every situation, by prayer and petition, with thanksgiving, present your requests to God. And the peace of God, which transcends all understanding, will guard your hearts and your minds in Christ Jesus."** I pray for Your peace to fill my heart and mind as I prepare for this job interview. Help me to trust in Your plan for my life and to rely on Your strength in every moment.

Father, I ask for wisdom and discernment as I navigate this interview process. Your Word tells us in **James 1:5, "If any of you lacks wisdom, you should ask God, who gives generously to all without finding fault, and it will be given to you."** Grant me the wisdom to answer questions with clarity and confidence, and to present myself in the best possible light.

I also pray for favor in the eyes of the interviewers. Your Word assures us in **Proverbs 3:4, "Then you will win favor and a good name in the sight of God and man."** May I be seen as a strong candidate for the position and may Your favor rest upon me throughout the interview process.

Lord, I commit this job interview into Your hands, trusting in Your perfect timing and provision. May Your will be done in my life, and may this opportunity be aligned with Your plans for my future. Help me to remain calm and focused, knowing that You are with me every step of the way.

In Jesus' name I pray,
Amen.

Prayer for
Journey Mercy

Heavenly Father,

As we embark on this journey, we come before You with hearts full of gratitude for Your goodness and protection in our lives. Your Word assures us in **Psalm 121:8, "The Lord will watch over your coming and going both now and forevermore."** We thank You for Your promise to accompany us wherever we go.

Lord, we pray for journey mercy as we travel. Your Word in **Psalm 91:11-12** reminds us, **"For he will command his angels concerning you to guard you in all your ways; they will lift you up in their hands, so that you will not strike your foot against a stone."** We ask that You send Your angels to surround our vehicle and guide us safely to our destination.

Father, we ask for protection against all forms of danger and harm along the way. Shield us from accidents, breakdowns, and any unforeseen obstacles. Your Word in **Isaiah 43:2** reassures us, **"When you pass through the waters, I will be with you; and when you pass through the rivers, they will not sweep over you. When you walk through the fire, you will not be burned; the flames will not set you ablaze."**

Lord, we also pray for peace and calmness throughout the journey. May Your presence be felt in our midst, calming any fears or anxieties. Your Word in **Philippians 4:7** declares, **"And the peace of God, which transcends all understanding, will guard your hearts and your minds in Christ Jesus."** Grant us Your peace that surpasses all understanding.

Father, we commit this journey into Your hands, trusting in Your unfailing love and protection. Guide us safely to our destination, and may our hearts be filled with gratitude and praise for Your faithfulness.

In Jesus' name, we pray,
Amen.

Prayer for
Justice

Heavenly Father,

I come before You seeking justice in a world that often seems unjust. Your Word teaches us in **Micah 6:8** to act justly, to love mercy, and to walk humbly with You. Help me, Lord, to embody these principles in my own life and to advocate for justice in the world around me.

Father, You are the ultimate source of justice. **Psalm 89:14** tells us that righteousness and justice are the foundation of Your throne, and steadfast love and faithfulness go before You. I pray that You would establish justice in every corner of the earth, that the oppressed may be set free and the marginalized may be lifted up.

Lord, You are a God of truth and justice. **Psalm 33:5** declares that You love righteousness and justice, and the earth is full of Your unfailing love. I ask that You guide the leaders and authorities of this world to govern with justice and integrity, so that all people may experience the blessings of Your justice.

Father, I lift up those who have been wronged or oppressed. Your Word promises in **Isaiah 61:8** that You love justice and hate robbery and wrongdoing. Bring comfort and healing to those who have suffered injustice, and may they find hope and restoration in Your unfailing love.

Lord, help me to be an agent of justice in my own sphere of influence. Give me the courage to speak out against injustice, the compassion to stand with the oppressed, and the wisdom to seek solutions that are rooted in Your truth and righteousness.

May Your kingdom come and Your will be done on earth as it is in heaven, where justice reigns forevermore.

In Jesus' name, I pray,
Amen.

Prayer for
Kindness

Heavenly Father,

We come before You with grateful hearts, acknowledging Your boundless love and kindness toward us. Your Word in **Ephesians 4:32** instructs us, **"Be kind and compassionate to one another, forgiving each other, just as in Christ God forgave you."** We pray that You would fill our hearts with Your kindness so that we may reflect Your love to others.

Lord, help us to see others through Your eyes, recognizing their worth and treating them with compassion and kindness. Your Word in **Luke 6:31** reminds us, **"Do to others as you would have them do to you."** May we extend the same kindness to others that we would desire for ourselves.

Grant us, O Lord, the humility to serve others with kindness, following the example of Your Son, Jesus Christ. Your Word in **Philippians 2:3-4** teaches us, **"Do nothing out of selfish ambition or vain conceit. Rather, in humility value others above yourselves, not looking to your own interests but each of you to the interests of the others."** May we prioritize the needs of others and seek opportunities to show kindness in both word and deed.

Father, we pray for the strength to overcome selfishness and pride, which hinder our ability to show kindness. Your Word in **Galatians 5:22-23** tells us, **"But the fruit of the Spirit is love, joy, peace, forbearance, kindness, goodness, faithfulness, gentleness and self-control. Against such things there is no law."** May Your Spirit produce in us the fruit of kindness, enabling us to bless others and bring glory to Your name.

Lord, we also ask for discernment to recognize opportunities to show kindness, even in the midst of challenges and trials. Your Word in **Colossians 3:12** encourages us, **"Therefore, as God's chosen people, holy and dearly loved, clothe yourselves with compassion, kIndness, humility, gentleness and patience."** May kindness be a garment we wear daily, reflecting Your character to a world in need.

We surrender our hearts to You, Lord, asking that You would fill us with Your kindness and empower us to be agents of Your love and grace in the lives of others. May our acts of kindness point others to You, the source of all kindness and compassion.

In Jesus' name we pray,
Amen.

Prayer for
Leadership Skills

Heavenly Father,

We come before You today seeking Your guidance and wisdom as we pray for leadership skills. Your Word teaches us in **James 1:5, "If any of you lacks wisdom, you should ask God, who gives generously to all without finding fault, and it will be given to you."** We humbly ask for Your wisdom to lead others with integrity, humility, and grace. Lord, You are the ultimate example of leadership, as Jesus Himself said in **Mark 10:45, "For even the Son of Man did not come to be served, but to serve, and to give his life as a ransom for many."** Teach us to lead by serving others, just as Jesus did, putting the needs of others before our own desires.

Grant us discernment, O Lord, to make wise decisions that align with Your will and bring glory to Your name. **Proverbs 3:5-6** reminds us, **"Trust in the Lord with all your heart and lean not on your own understanding; in all your ways submit to him, and he will make your paths straight."** Help us to trust in You completely and to seek Your guidance in all aspects of leadership.

Father, we pray for humility in leadership, knowing that pride goes before destruction, as **Proverbs 16:18** tells us. Help us to lead with humility, recognizing that all authority comes from You, and that our ultimate goal is to serve and honor You in everything we do.

Equip us with patience and perseverance, Lord, as we navigate the challenges of leadership. Your Word encourages us in **Galatians 6:9, "Let us not become weary in doing good, for at the proper time we will reap a harvest if we do not give up."** Give us strength to persevere through trials and to remain steadfast in our commitment to lead with excellence.

Finally, Lord, we pray for courage to lead with conviction and to stand firm in our faith. **Joshua 1:9** assures us, **"Be strong and courageous. Do not be afraid; do not be discouraged, for the Lord your God will be with you wherever you go."** May we be bold in our leadership, knowing that You are with us every step of the way. We commit our leadership roles into Your hands, Lord, trusting in Your provision and guidance. May our leadership skills be a reflection of Your love, wisdom, and grace, drawing others closer to You and bringing glory to Your name.

In Jesus' name, we pray,
Amen.

Prayer for Learning The Word of God

Heavenly Father,

I come before You with a humble and eager heart, desiring to grow in my knowledge and understanding of Your Word. **Psalm 119:105** reminds me that Your Word is a lamp to my feet and a light to my path, and I long to immerse myself in its truth.

Lord, I ask for Your guidance and wisdom as I delve into the Scriptures. As written in **Psalm 119:18**, open my eyes to see the wonderful things in Your law and grant me understanding as I study and meditate on Your Word.

Father, Your Word tells us in **James 1:5, "If any of you lacks wisdom, you should ask God, who gives generously to all without finding fault, and it will be given to you."**

I humbly ask for Your wisdom to comprehend the depths of Your truth and to apply it to my life.

Help me to approach Your Word with humility, reverence, and a teachable spirit. May I be like the Bereans, who examined the Scriptures every day to see if what they heard was true as written in **Acts 17:11**. Grant me discernment to rightly divide the word of truth.

Lord, I pray that Your Holy Spirit would be my teacher and guide as I study Your Word. Illuminate the Scriptures to me and reveal Your will and purposes for my life through its pages.

Father, I commit myself to regular and disciplined study of Your Word, knowing that it is living and active, sharper than any double-edged sword as written in **Hebrews 4:12**. May Your Word dwell richly in me, transforming my heart and mind according to Your perfect will.

In Jesus' name I pray,
Amen.

Prayer for Loneliness

Heavenly Father,

In moments of loneliness and isolation, we come before You, seeking Your presence and comfort. Your Word reminds us in **Psalm 23:4, "Even though I walk through the darkest valley, I will fear no evil, for you are with me; your rod and your staff, they comfort me."** We take solace in knowing that You are with us, even in our loneliest moments.

Lord, we bring before You the ache of our hearts and the longing for companionship. You understand our deepest desires and our need for connection, for You created us for fellowship with You and with one another.

Father, help us to find our ultimate fulfillment and satisfaction in You alone. Your Word declares in **Psalm 73:25-26, "Whom have I in heaven but you? And earth has nothing I desire besides you. My flesh and my heart may fail, but God is the strength of my heart and my portion forever."** May we find our true refuge and strength in You, even in the midst of loneliness.

Lord, we ask for Your comfort to surround us like a warm embrace. Help us to sense Your presence with us, bringing peace to our troubled hearts and assurance to our weary souls.

Father, remind us of the love and community You have provided through Your church and Your people. Help us to reach out to others and to build meaningful connections, knowing that we are not alone but part of Your family.

Lord, we surrender our feelings of loneliness into Your hands, trusting that You are our ever-present companion who walks with us through every season of life.

Father, we thank You for Your faithfulness and Your promise never to leave us nor forsake us as reassured in **Hebrews 13:5**. May Your love fill the emptiness within us and Your presence bring us the peace that surpasses all understanding.

In Jesus' name, we pray,
Amen.

Prayer for Love

Heavenly Father,

You are the source of all love, and Your Word tells us that You are love. As written in **1 John 4:8, "Whoever does not love does not know God, because God is love."** I come before You now, Lord, to seek Your guidance and strength in understanding and embodying the true essence of love.

Father, Your Word teaches us that love is patient and kind. Help me to cultivate patience and kindness in my heart according to **1 Corinthians 13:4**, especially towards those who may be difficult to love. Teach me to extend grace and compassion to others, just as You have shown me.

Lord, Your love is unconditional and sacrificial. You demonstrated the depth of Your love for us by sending Your Son, Jesus Christ, to die for our sins. Help me to love others selflessly, putting their needs above my own and seeking their well-being. Father, Your Word in **John 13:34**, commands us to love one another as You have loved us. I pray for the grace to love my neighbor as myself, showing kindness, generosity, and forgiveness to all those around me. May my actions and words reflect the love that You have poured into my heart.

Lord, I confess that I often fall short in loving others as I should. Forgive me for moments of selfishness, pride, and indifference. Fill me with Your Holy Spirit so that I may love with the same depth and purity that You have loved me.

Father, I pray for unity and harmony among Your children, that we may be known by our love for one another as written in **John 17:23**. Help us to set aside differences and grievances, and to embrace each other with genuine affection and compassion.

Lord, I ask for Your love to abound more and more in my life, overflowing into every relationship and every interaction. May Your love be the driving force behind all that I do, bringing glory to Your name and drawing others closer to You.

Thank You, Father, for the immeasurable love You have lavished upon me. May I never take Your love for granted, but instead, may it compel me to love others fervently and faithfully.

In Jesus' name, I pray,
Amen.

Prayer for
Lust

Heavenly Father,

We come before You with humble hearts, acknowledging our struggles and weaknesses. Your Word reminds us in **1 Corinthians 10:13, "No temptation has overtaken you except what is common to mankind. And God is faithful; he will not let you be tempted beyond what you can bear. But when you are tempted, he will also provide a way out so that you can endure it."** We confess our struggle with lust and our need for Your strength to overcome it.

Lord, we recognize that lust is a distortion of Your gift of sexuality, intended to be expressed within the bounds of marriage and love. Your Word instructs us in **1 Thessalonians 4:3-5, "It is God's will that you should be sanctified: that you should avoid sexual immorality; that each of you should learn to control your own body in a way that is holy and honorable, not in passionate lust like the pagans, who do not know God."** Help us to honor Your design for sexuality and to flee from lustful desires.

Father, we repent of any ways in which we have indulged in lustful thoughts, actions, or behaviors. Your Word warns us in **Matthew 5:28, "But I tell you that anyone who looks at a woman lustfully has already committed adultery with her in his heart."**

Forgive us for dishonoring You and others through our sinful desires. Create in us clean hearts, O God, and renew a steadfast spirit within us as written in **Psalm 51:10**. Lord, we pray for Your Spirit to empower us to resist the temptation of lust and to walk in purity and holiness. Your Word assures us in **Romans 8:5, "Those who live according to the flesh have their minds set on what the flesh desires; but those who live in accordance with the Spirit have their minds set on what the Spirit desires."** Help us to fix our eyes on You and to pursue righteousness with all our hearts.

Father, we ask for Your grace to fill our minds and hearts with thoughts that are pure, lovely, and honorable. Your Word encourages us in **Philippians 4:8, "Finally, brothers and sisters, whatever is true, whatever is noble, whatever is right, whatever is pure, whatever is lovely, whatever is admirable—if anything is excellent or praiseworthy—think about such things."**

Prayer for
Lust

May our thoughts be aligned with Your truth and our desires be directed towards that which is pleasing to You. Lord, we thank You for Your faithfulness to forgive us and to cleanse us from all unrighteousness when we confess our sins to You as promised in **1 John 1:9**. Strengthen us to walk in purity and to resist the allure of lustful temptations. Help us to find our satisfaction and fulfillment in You alone, knowing that You are the true source of joy and contentment.

In Jesus' name, we pray,
Amen.

Prayer for
Marriage or Wedding

Heavenly Father,

We come before You today with hearts full of gratitude for the gift of marriage, a sacred union ordained by You from the beginning of time. We thank You for the love that **[Couple's Names]** share, and for the commitment they have made to one another. As it is written in **Genesis 2:24, "That is why a man leaves his father and mother and is united to his wife, and they become one flesh."**

Lord, we pray for **[Couple's Names]** as they embark on this journey together. May their marriage be built upon the foundation of Your love, grace, and truth. Help them to honor and cherish one another, to support and encourage each other, and to grow together in faith and unity. As it is written in **Ecclesiastes 4:9-10, "Two are better than one, because they have a good return for their labor: If either of them falls down, one can help the other up. But pity anyone who falls and has no one to help them up."**

Grant them wisdom, O Lord, as they navigate the joys and challenges of married life. May they always seek Your guidance in their decisions and rely on Your strength to sustain them through every season. As it is written in **Proverbs 3:5-6, "Trust in the Lord with all your heart and lean not on your own understanding; in all your ways submit to him, and he will make your paths straight."**

We pray for a bond of trust and communication to deepen between **[Couple's Names]**, that they may always be open and honest with one another. Help them to forgive as You have forgiven them, to extend grace and mercy to one another, and to choose love above all else. As it is written in **Colossians 3:13, "Bear with each other and forgive one another if any of you has a grievance against someone. Forgive as the Lord forgave you."**

Lord, we also lift up their families and loved ones who rejoice with them in this union. May they offer support, encouragement, and prayers for **[Couple's Names]** as they embark on this new chapter of their lives together.

May their marriage be a testament to Your faithfulness and goodness, bringing glory to Your name and reflecting Your love to the world. Bless their home with joy, peace, and abundant blessings.

In Jesus' name we pray,
Amen.

Prayer for
Managers and Supervisors

Heavenly Father,

I come before You today with a heart full of gratitude for the blessing of having a manager or supervisor in my life. Your Word in **Colossians 3:23-24** reminds me, **"Whatever you do, work at it with all your heart, as working for the Lord, not for human masters, since you know that you will receive an inheritance from the Lord as a reward. It is the Lord Christ you are serving."**

Lord, I lift up my manager/supervisor to You, acknowledging their role in my life and the authority You have placed upon them. I pray that You would grant them wisdom, discernment, and strength as they lead and oversee the work entrusted to them. May they be guided by Your Spirit in their decisions and actions, always seeking to honor You in all that they do.

Father, I ask for harmony and understanding in our working relationship. Help me to respect and honor my manager/supervisor, recognizing their authority as ordained by You. Your Word in **Romans 13:1** reminds me, **"Let everyone be subject to the governing authorities, for there is no authority except that which God has established. The authorities that exist have been established by God."**

Grant us the grace to communicate effectively and to work together in unity and cooperation. May our interactions be marked by grace, humility, and mutual respect, reflecting Your love and grace to those around us. Your Word in **Ephesians 4:2-3** instructs me, **"Be completely humble and gentle; be patient, bearing with one another in love. Make every effort to keep the unity of the Spirit through the bond of peace."**

Lord, I pray for my manager/supervisor's well-being and success. Bless them with good health, peace of mind, and joy in their work. May they find fulfillment and satisfaction in their role, knowing that they are serving You in all that they do.

I commit our working relationship into Your hands, trusting in Your wisdom and sovereignty. May our interactions bring glory to Your name and be a testimony to Your grace and goodness.

In Jesus' name I pray,
Amen.

Prayer for
Mercy

Heavenly Father,

I come before You humbly, acknowledging Your boundless mercy and compassion. Your Word teaches us in **Lamentations 3:22-23** that Your mercies are new every morning; great is Your faithfulness. Lord, I thank You for Your unfailing love and Your willingness to extend mercy to those who seek You.

You have shown us the depth of Your mercy through Your Son, Jesus Christ, who died on the cross to redeem us from our sins. As it says in **Ephesians 2:4-5, "But because of his great love for us, God, who is rich in mercy, made us alive with Christ even when we were dead in transgressions—it is by grace you have been saved."**

Father, I confess that I am in need of Your mercy each day. I have fallen short of Your glory and have sinned against You. Yet, I am grateful for the promise of forgiveness and restoration found in Your mercy.

I pray, Lord, that You would pour out Your mercy upon me, covering my sins and cleansing me from all unrighteousness. Help me to truly repent and turn away from any attitudes, actions, or thoughts that are not pleasing to You.

Father, I also ask for Your mercy to be evident in my relationships with others. Grant me the grace to forgive those who have wronged me, just as You have forgiven me. Help me to show compassion and kindness to those in need, reflecting Your mercy to the world around me.

Lord, I pray for Your mercy to be evident in our world today, especially in times of suffering, injustice, and strife. Bring healing, reconciliation, and peace to those who are hurting, and may Your mercy lead many to repentance and salvation.

Thank You, Lord, for Your abundant mercy that endures forever. May I always seek to walk in humility and gratitude, trusting in Your mercy and grace to sustain me each day.

In Jesus' name, I pray,
Amen.

Prayer for Ministry

Heavenly Father,

We come before You today with hearts full of gratitude for the privilege of serving in Your kingdom and for the opportunity to be vessels of Your love and grace through our ministry. Your word tells us in **Ephesians 2:10, "For we are God's handiwork, created in Christ Jesus to do good works, which God prepared in advance for us to do."** Thank You for calling us to this work and for equipping us with the gifts and talents needed to fulfill Your purposes.

Lord, we pray for our ministry. May it be guided by Your Holy Spirit and grounded in Your word. Help us to always seek Your will and to align our efforts with Your purposes. Your word also tells us in **Proverbs 3:5-6, "Trust in the Lord with all your heart and lean not on your own understanding; in all your ways submit to him, and he will make your paths straight."** May our ministry reflect Your love and compassion, reaching out to those in need and sharing the hope found in Jesus Christ.

Father, we pray for wisdom, discernment, and strength as we carry out the work of this ministry. Grant us clarity of vision and direction and help us to prioritize what is most important in advancing Your kingdom. Your word reminds us in **James 1:5, "If any of you lacks wisdom, you should ask God, who gives generously to all without finding fault, and it will be given to you."** May we be faithful stewards of the resources and opportunities You have entrusted to us.

Lord, we lift up those whom we serve through this ministry. May they encounter Your presence and experience Your transforming power in their lives. Your word tells us in **Isaiah 40:31, "But those who hope in the Lord will renew their strength. They will soar on wings like eagles; they will run and not grow weary; they will walk and not be faint."** Use us as instruments of Your grace and mercy, bringing healing, restoration, and hope to those who are hurting and broken.

Father, we ask for Your protection and provision over our ministry. Guard us against the attacks of the enemy and provide for our every need according to Your riches in glory. Your word assures us in **Philippians 4:19, "And my God will meet all your needs according to the riches of his glory in Christ Jesus."** We commit our ministry into Your hands, trusting in Your faithfulness to guide, protect, and empower us to fulfill Your purposes and to bring glory to Your name. As we continue to serve, may all glory and honor be unto You.

In Jesus' name we pray,
Amen.

Prayer for
Miracle

Heavenly Father,

I come before You with a humble heart, acknowledging Your power to work miracles in our lives. Your Word tells us in **Mark 10:27, "Jesus looked at them and said, 'With man this is impossible, but not with God; all things are possible with God.'"** I believe in Your power to perform miracles, and I lift up my request to You.

Lord, as You have said in **Jeremiah 32:27**, You are the God of miracles, and nothing is too difficult for You. I bring before You my deepest need and ask for Your intervention. You are the same yesterday, today, and forever as written in **Hebrews 13:8**, and I trust in Your faithfulness to answer my prayers according to Your will.

Father, I pray for *[DESCRIBE THE SPECIFIC MIRACLE NEEDED]*.

I know that You are able to do exceedingly abundantly above all that we ask or think, according to the power that works in us as written in **Ephesians 3:20**. Please work in my life in a miraculous way, bringing glory to Your name and demonstrating Your love and compassion.

Lord, Your Word tells us in **Matthew 7:7-8, "Ask and it will be given to you; seek and you will find; knock and the door will be opened to you. For everyone who asks receives; the one who seeks finds; and to the one who knocks, the door will be opened."** I come before You with faith, asking, seeking, and knocking, trusting in Your promises.

I surrender my will to Yours, knowing that Your plans for me are good and perfect as assured in **Romans 12:2**. Help me to trust in Your timing and to remain steadfast in prayer as I wait for Your miraculous intervention.

Lord, I commit this request into Your hands, confident in Your ability to do far more than I could ever imagine. May Your will be done, and may Your name be glorified through this miracle.

In Jesus' name I pray,
Amen.

Prayer for Missionaries

Heavenly Father,

We come before You with hearts full of gratitude for the courageous men and women who have dedicated their lives to spreading Your Gospel to the ends of the earth. Your Word instructs us in **Matthew 28:19-20, "Therefore go and make disciples of all nations, baptizing them in the name of the Father and of the Son and of the Holy Spirit, and teaching them to obey everything I have commanded you. And surely I am with you always, to the very end of the age."** We lift up missionaries everywhere, asking for Your divine guidance, protection, and provision as they fulfill the Great Commission.

Lord, we pray for strength and endurance for missionaries as they face the challenges and obstacles of cross-cultural ministry. Your Word assures us in **Isaiah 40:31, "but those who hope in the Lord will renew their strength. They will soar on wings like eagles; they will run and not grow weary, they will walk and not be faint."** Renew their strength, Lord, and empower them to persevere in their mission with unwavering faith.

Father, we ask for Your divine protection over missionaries and their families as they serve in areas that may be hostile to the Gospel. Your Word promises in **Psalm 91:11-12, "For he will command his angels concerning you to guard you in all your ways; they will lift you up in their hands, so that you will not strike your foot against a stone."** Surround them with Your heavenly angels, Lord, and keep them safe from harm.

Lord Jesus, we pray for open doors and receptive hearts among the people to whom missionaries are ministering. Your Word declares in **Revelation 3:8, "I know your deeds. See, I have placed before you an open door that no one can shut. I know that you have little strength, yet you have kept my word and have not denied my name."** Open doors of opportunity for Your Word to be preached and received, Lord, and soften the hearts of those who hear it.

Father, we pray for provision for the practical needs of missionaries and their families. Your Word assures us in **Philippians 4:19, "And my God will meet all your needs according to the riches of his glory in Christ Jesus."** Provide for their financial, emotional, and physical needs, Lord, and grant them peace and contentment in Your provision.

Prayer for Missionaries

Lord, we lift up the spiritual well-being of missionaries, asking for Your anointing and empowerment as they proclaim Your Word. Your Word declares in **Acts 1:8, "But you will receive power when the Holy Spirit comes on you; and you will be my witnesses in Jerusalem, and in all Judea and Samaria, and to the ends of the earth."** Fill them afresh with Your Holy Spirit, Lord, and use them as powerful witnesses for Your kingdom.

Father, we pray for fruitfulness and effectiveness in the ministry of missionaries, that many souls may be saved and disciples may be made for Your glory. Your Word assures us in **Isaiah 55:11, "so is my word that goes out from my mouth: It will not return to me empty, but will accomplish what I desire and achieve the purpose for which I sent it."** Let Your Word go forth with power and authority, Lord, and bring forth a harvest of souls.

Lord, we commit missionaries into Your hands, trusting in Your faithfulness to equip, protect, and empower them as they fulfill Your Great Commission. May their lives be a living testimony to Your love and grace, and may the nations come to know You through their ministry.

In Jesus' name, we pray,
Amen.

Prayer for
Morning - new day

Heavenly Father,

As I open my eyes to greet a new day, I come before You with a heart full of gratitude for the gift of life and the opportunity to experience Your mercy and grace afresh. Your Word in **Lamentations 3:22-23** reminds me, **"Because of the Lord's great love we are not consumed, for his compassions never fail. They are new every morning; great is your faithfulness."**

Lord, I thank You for the restful sleep You have granted me and for the protection You provided through the night. I commit this new day into Your hands, trusting in Your guidance and provision. Your Word in **Psalm 143:8** says, **"Let the morning bring me word of your unfailing love, for I have put my trust in you. Show me the way I should go, for to you I entrust my life."**

Father, I ask for Your presence to be with me throughout this day. May Your Holy Spirit guide my thoughts, words, and actions, leading me in the paths of righteousness. Help me to be mindful of Your will and to walk in obedience to Your Word. Your Word in **Proverbs 3:5-6** instructs me, **"Trust in the Lord with all your heart and lean not on your own understanding; in all your ways submit to him, and he will make your paths straight."**

Grant me wisdom and discernment as I navigate the challenges and opportunities that come my way. May I honor You in all that I do, reflecting Your love and grace to those around me. Your Word in **Colossians 3:17** reminds me, **"And whatever you do, whether in word or deed, do it all in the name of the Lord Jesus, giving thanks to God the Father through him."**

Lord, I surrender myself into Your loving care, knowing that You are faithful to uphold me and sustain me throughout this day. May I be a vessel of Your light and truth, sharing Your love with others and bringing glory to Your holy name.

In Jesus' name I pray,
Amen.

Prayer for Mother

Heavenly Father,

I come before You today with a heart full of gratitude for the gift of my mother, *[Mother's Name]*. Thank You for her love, care, and sacrifices she has made for me throughout my life. I lift her up to You now, knowing that You are the source of all comfort, strength, and grace. As it is written in **Proverbs 31:28, "Her children arise and call her blessed; her husband also, and he praises her."**

Lord, I pray for my mother's health and well-being. Grant her physical strength, emotional peace, and mental clarity. Surround her with Your healing presence and may any pain or concerns she carries be lifted by Your loving touch. As it is written in **Psalm 41:3, "The Lord sustains them on their sickbed and restores them from their bed of illness."**

Father, I also pray for my mother's spiritual journey. Draw her closer to You each day, deepening her faith and trust in Your goodness and mercy. May she find joy and fulfillment in her relationship with You and be a shining example of Your love to those around her. As it is written in **James 4:8, "Come near to God and he will come near to you."**

Guide my mother in her roles and responsibilities as a wife, mother, and friend. Give her wisdom and discernment in decision-making, and help her to lead our family with grace, compassion, and wisdom. As it is written in **Proverbs 3:5-6, "Trust in the Lord with all your heart and lean not on your own understanding; in all your ways submit to him, and he will make your paths straight."**

Lord, I ask for Your protection over my mother, both physically and spiritually. Guard her against harm and keep her safe from the schemes of the enemy. Surround her with Your angels and cover her with Your peace. As it is written in **Psalm 91:11-12, "For he will command his angels concerning you to guard you in all your ways; they will lift you up in their hands, so that you will not strike your foot against a stone."**

As I honor my mother today, I thank You for the ways she has shaped me and influenced my life. May she feel deeply loved and appreciated, not just today but every day. I commit my mother into Your loving hands, trusting in Your faithfulness to watch over her and to guide her in all her ways.

In Jesus' name I pray,
Amen.

Prayer for
Neighbour

Heavenly Father,

I come before You with a heart full of love and concern for my neighbor, *[Neighbor's Name]*. Your Word teaches us in **Mark 12:31, "Love your neighbor as yourself."** Lord, help me to fulfill this commandment by lifting up *[Neighbor's Name]* in prayer today.

Father, I pray for *[Neighbor's Name]'s* well-being, both physically and spiritually. May Your hand be upon them, guiding and protecting them in all aspects of their life. I ask that You would grant them good health, peace of mind, and strength for the journey ahead.

Lord, I also pray for *[Neighbor's Name]'s* spiritual journey. Draw them closer to You, opening their eyes to Your love and truth. Your Word in **Ephesians 1:18 says, "I pray that the eyes of your heart may be enlightened in order that you may know the hope to which he has called you, the riches of his glorious inheritance in his holy people."**

May *[Neighbor's Name]* come to know the hope and salvation found in Jesus Christ, experiencing the transformational power of Your grace.

Father, help me to be a good neighbor to *[Neighbor's Name]*, showing kindness, compassion, and generosity. Give me opportunities to share Your love with them through both words and deeds, that they may see Your light shining through me.

Lord, I commit *[Neighbor's Name]* into Your loving hands, trusting in Your perfect plan and timing for their life. May Your will be done in their life, and may they come to know You as their Savior and Lord.

In Jesus' name, I pray,
Amen.

Prayer for
Obedience

Heavenly Father,

I come before You with a humble heart, acknowledging Your sovereignty and lordship over my life. Your Word in **1 Samuel 15:22** reminds us, **"To obey is better than sacrifice, and to heed is better than the fat of rams."** Lord, I desire to obey Your commands wholeheartedly, knowing that obedience is the pathway to blessings and favor in Your sight.

Forgive me, Lord, for the times when I have fallen short of obeying Your will. Help me to surrender my own desires and preferences to Your perfect plan for my life. Your Word in **Romans 6:16** teaches us, **"Don't you know that when you offer yourselves to someone as obedient slaves, you are slaves of the one you obey—whether you are slaves to sin, which leads to death, or to obedience, which leads to righteousness?"** May I choose obedience to You, Lord, recognizing that it leads to righteousness and life.

Grant me the strength and courage to obey You even when it is difficult or inconvenient. Your Word in **Joshua 1:9** encourages us, **"Have I not commanded you? Be strong and courageous. Do not be afraid; do not be discouraged, for the Lord your God will be with you wherever you go."** Help me to trust in Your presence and to step out in obedience, knowing that You are with me every step of the way.

I pray for a heart that is sensitive to Your voice and promptings. Your Word in **John 14:15** reminds us, **"If you love me, keep my commands."** Lord, help me to love You more deeply each day, so that my obedience flows out of a heart of love and devotion to You.

Thank You, Lord, for Your patience and grace towards me. Your Word in **Psalm 119:105** declares, **"Your word is a lamp for my feet, a light on my path."** May Your Word guide my steps and illuminate the path of obedience before me.

I surrender my will to Yours, Lord, and ask for the empowerment of Your Holy Spirit to walk in obedience each day. May my life bring glory and honor to Your name as I seek to follow You faithfully.

In Jesus' name, I pray,
Amen.

Prayer for
Opening Prayer

Heavenly Father,

We come before You today with hearts full of gratitude for the gift of community and the privilege of prayer. Thank You for bringing us together as a prayer group, where we can support and uplift one another in faith. As it is written in **Matthew 18:20, "For where two or three gather in my name, there am I with them."**

We ask for Your presence to be with us as we gather in Your name. Pour out Your Spirit upon us, filling us with love, wisdom, and understanding. Help us to be sensitive to Your voice and obedient to Your will. As it is written in **Ephesians 5:18, "Do not get drunk on wine, which leads to debauchery. Instead, be filled with the Spirit."**

Lord, we lift up our intentions and needs to You. You know the desires of our hearts and the challenges we face. Grant us strength to overcome obstacles, faith to believe in Your promises, and courage to walk in obedience to Your word. As it is written in **Philippians 4:13, "I can do all this through him who gives me strength."**

We pray for unity and harmony within our group. May our interactions be marked by grace, compassion, and mutual respect. Heal any divisions or misunderstandings among us and help us to forgive as You have forgiven us. As it is written in **Colossians 3:13, "Bear with each other and forgive one another if any of you has a grievance against someone. Forgive as the Lord forgave you."**

Father, we intercede for others who are in need. We lift up the sick, the suffering, the lonely, and the oppressed. May Your healing touch be upon them, and may they experience Your comfort and peace in their time of need. As it is written in **James 5:16, "Therefore confess your sins to each other and pray for each other so that you may be healed. The prayer of a righteous person is powerful and effective."**

Guide us, O Lord, in the paths of righteousness. Lead us to walk in Your ways and to shine Your light in a world filled with darkness. Give us the courage to be Your hands and feet, sharing Your love with those around us. We surrender our prayers and our lives into Your hands, trusting in Your goodness and faithfulness. May Your kingdom come and Your will be done on earth as it is in heaven.

In Jesus' name we pray,
Amen.

Prayer for Opportunities

Heavenly Father,

I come before You with gratitude for the opportunities You have placed before me, knowing that every good gift comes from You, as stated in **James 1:17**. You are the God who opens doors and makes a way where there seems to be no way. I thank You for the doors of opportunity that You have already opened in my life, and I pray for the wisdom to recognize and seize the opportunities that You continue to present to me.

Lord, Your Word tells me in **Psalm 37:4** that if I delight myself in You, You will give me the desires of my heart. Help me to delight in You above all else, seeking first Your kingdom and Your righteousness, as instructed in **Matthew 6:33**. As I align my desires with Your will, I trust that You will guide me into the opportunities that are in accordance with Your plan for my life.

Father, I pray for discernment to recognize the opportunities that You have ordained for me and the courage to pursue them wholeheartedly. Your Word assures me in **Ephesians 5:15-16** to be careful how I live, not as unwise but as wise, making the most of every opportunity, because the days are evil. May I seize each opportunity as a chance to glorify You and advance Your kingdom here on earth.

Lord, I also pray for patience and perseverance as I wait for the opportunities that are yet to come. Help me to trust in Your timing and to remain faithful in prayer, knowing that You are always working behind the scenes for my good, as stated in **Romans 8:28**.

Thank You, Lord, for the promise of abundant life that You have given to me through Jesus Christ. May I walk in the confidence of knowing that You are with me, guiding me and providing for me each step of the way.

In Jesus' name, I pray,
Amen.

Prayer for
Passion and Purpose

Heavenly Father,

I come before You with a heart full of gratitude for the passions and purposes You have placed within me. Your Word tells me in **Psalm 139:13-14** that You knit me together in my mother's womb and that I am fearfully and wonderfully made.

Thank You for creating me with unique talents, gifts, and passions designed to fulfill the purpose You have ordained for my life.

Lord, I seek Your guidance and wisdom as I discern my passions and pursue my purpose. Your Word reminds me in **Proverbs 3:5-6** to trust in You with all my heart and lean not on my own understanding, but in all my ways acknowledge You, and You will direct my paths. May I trust in Your plan for my life and surrender my desires to Your will.

Father, help me to align my passions with Your purposes and to use my gifts and abilities to glorify You and bless others. Your Word teaches me in **Romans 12:6-8** that each of us has different gifts, according to the grace given to us, so let me use them accordingly, whether it be serving, teaching, encouraging, giving, leading, or showing mercy.

Lord, I pray for clarity and direction as I seek to fulfill the purpose You have called me to. Your Word assures me in **Jeremiah 29:11** that You have plans for me, plans to prosper me and not to harm me, plans to give me hope and a future. May I walk confidently in the assurance of Your promises, knowing that You are always with me.

Thank You, Lord, for the passion and purpose You have placed within me. May my life be a reflection of Your love, grace, and mercy, as I seek to fulfill the calling You have placed on my life.

In Jesus' name, I pray,
Amen.

Prayer for
Pastor

Heavenly Father,

We come before You today with hearts full of gratitude for the gift of our pastor. Thank You for the servant-hearted leadership *[NAME]* provides to our congregation and the love he/she pours out to shepherd Your flock.

As it is written in **Ephesians 4:11-12, "So Christ himself gave the apostles, the prophets, the evangelists, the pastors and teachers, to equip his people for works of service, so that the body of Christ may be built up."**

Lord, we lift up our pastor to You, asking for Your continued guidance, wisdom, and strength as *he/she* fulfills the calling You have placed upon *his/her* life. Grant *him/her* the wisdom to rightly divide Your word, wisdom to navigate the challenges of ministry, and courage to stand firm in their convictions. As it is written in **James 1:5, "If any of you lacks wisdom, you should ask God, who gives generously to all without finding fault, and it will be given to you."**

Bless our pastor with good health, both physically and spiritually. Refresh *him/her* with Your Spirit daily, renewing *his/her* strength and passion for ministry. Surround *him/her* with Your protection against the plans of the enemy and guard *his/her* heart and mind with Your peace. As it is written in **Psalm 28:7, "The Lord is my strength and my shield; my heart trusts in him, and he helps me. My heart leaps for joy, and with my song I praise him."**

Father, we pray for our pastor's family as well. May they feel Your love and support in every season of life, and may their home be a place of refuge and joy. Strengthen the bonds of love between them and help them to prioritize their relationship with You and with one another. As it is written in **Joshua 24:15, "But as for me and my household, we will serve the Lord."**

Lord, we thank You for the ways *[NAME]* has impacted our lives and the lives of others. May *his/her* ministry bear much fruit for Your kingdom and may *he/she* hear You say "Well-done, my good and faithful servant" when *he/she* stands before You in eternity.

We commit our pastor into Your hands, trusting in Your faithfulness to sustain *him/her* and to fulfill every good work You have prepared for him/her to do.

In Jesus' name we pray,
Amen.

Prayer for
Patience

Heavenly Father,

We come before You, acknowledging Your sovereignty and wisdom. Your Word teaches us in **James 5:11, "As you know, we count as blessed those who have persevered. You have heard of Job's perseverance and have seen what the Lord finally brought about. The Lord is full of compassion and mercy."**

Lord, we confess that patience is a virtue that we often lack, yet it is essential for our growth and maturity in Christ. Teach us to wait upon You with trust and confidence, knowing that Your timing is perfect and Your ways are higher than ours as we are reminded in **Isaiah 55:8-9**.

Grant us patience in times of trials and tribulations, knowing that they produce endurance and ultimately lead to spiritual maturity as mentioned in **James 1:2-4**. Help us to count it all joy when we encounter various trials, knowing that the testing of our faith produces steadfastness.

Father, we pray for patience in our relationships, both with our loved ones and with those who may challenge us. Help us to bear with one another in love, being patient and kind, forgiving as You have forgiven us as instructed in **Ephesians 4:2-3**.

Lord Jesus, You are our ultimate example of patience. You endured suffering and persecution with patience and grace, never retaliating but entrusting Yourself to the Father who judges justly. Help us to follow in Your footsteps, enduring with patience whatever trials may come our way.

Holy Spirit, fill us with Your fruit of patience, enabling us to wait upon You with hope and expectancy. Help us to cultivate a patient heart that is slow to anger and quick to forgive, reflecting Your character to the world around us.

May patience be evident in every aspect of our lives, demonstrating Your transforming work within us. And may Your name be glorified as we learn to wait upon You with patience and perseverance.

In Jesus' name, we pray,
Amen.

Prayer for
Peace

Heavenly Father,

I come before You today seeking the peace that surpasses all understanding, as mentioned in **Philippians 4:7**. Lord, Your word assures us that You are the source of true peace, and I ask that You would fill my heart and mind with Your peace in every situation.

In the midst of turmoil and uncertainty, I look to You as my refuge and strength. Your word in **Isaiah 26:3** declares, **"You will keep in perfect peace those whose minds are steadfast because they trust in you."** Help me to trust in You completely, knowing that You are in control and that You work all things together for good for those who love You.

Lord, I pray for peace in my relationships, both with others and with myself. Your word teaches us in **Ephesians 4:3, "Make every effort to keep the unity of the Spirit through the bond of peace."** Help me to be a peacemaker, seeking reconciliation and understanding in all my interactions.

Father, I also lift up areas of conflict and division in the world. Your word tells us in **James 3:18, "Peacemakers who sow in peace reap a harvest of righteousness."** May Your peace reign in every nation and community, bringing unity and healing where there is discord and strife.

Lord, I ask for inner peace in the face of challenges and trials. Your word assures us in **John 16:33, "I have told you these things, so that in me you may have peace. In this world you will have trouble. But take heart! I have overcome the world."** Help me to find strength and courage in You, knowing that You are with me always.

Father, I surrender my worries, fears, and anxieties to You, trusting that You are able to calm the storms of life and bring peace to my soul. Your word in **Philippians 4:6** encourages us, **"Do not be anxious about anything, but in every situation, by prayer and petition, with thanksgiving, present your requests to God."** I lay my burdens before You and ask for Your peace to fill me afresh.

May Your peace, which transcends all understanding, guard my heart and mind in Christ Jesus.

In Jesus' name I pray,
Amen.

Prayer for Perserverance

Heavenly Father,

We come before You today, recognizing the challenges and obstacles that we face in this life. Your word reminds us in **James 1:12, "Blessed is the one who perseveres under trial because, having stood the test, that person will receive the crown of life that the Lord has promised to those who love him."** Lord, we seek Your strength and guidance to persevere through every trial and difficulty.

Grant us, O Lord, the perseverance to endure hardships with faith and patience. When we are tempted to give up or lose heart, remind us of Your promise to never leave us nor forsake us.

We pray for perseverance in our faith, Lord. Help us to hold fast to Your truth, even when the world around us may challenge or oppose it. Strengthen our resolve to follow You wholeheartedly, trusting in Your promises and walking in obedience to Your word.

Grant us perseverance in our relationships, Lord. Help us to love one another as You have loved us, even when it is difficult or inconvenient. Give us the grace to forgive, the humility to seek reconciliation, and the commitment to build and maintain healthy, loving connections with others.

We pray for perseverance in our work and service, Lord. Help us to remain steadfast and diligent, even when faced with setbacks or discouragement. Give us the perseverance to press on towards the goals You have set before us, knowing that our labor in the Lord is not in vain.

Lord, we ask for Your strength to endure and persevere through every trial and tribulation. May our perseverance be a testimony to Your faithfulness and grace, and may it ultimately bring glory to Your name.

In Jesus' name we pray,
Amen.

Prayer for
Poverty

Heavenly Father,

We come before You with hearts burdened by the plight of those who suffer under the weight of poverty and deprivation. Your Word teaches us in **Psalm 82:3-4, "Defend the weak and the fatherless; uphold the cause of the poor and the oppressed. Rescue the weak and the needy; deliver them from the hand of the wicked."**

We pray earnestly for an end to poverty and for Your justice to prevail in the lives of those who are marginalized and oppressed.

Lord, You are a God of compassion and mercy, and Your heart breaks for the poor and the needy. Your Word reminds us in **Proverbs 19:17, "Whoever is kind to the poor lends to the Lord, and he will reward them for what they have done."** We ask for Your provision to meet the material needs of the impoverished and for Your people to be instruments of Your love and generosity in alleviating their suffering.

Father, we pray for wisdom and discernment for leaders and policymakers as they address the systemic issues that perpetuate poverty. Your Word instructs us in **Isaiah 1:17, "Learn to do right; seek justice. Defend the oppressed. Take up the cause of the fatherless; plead the case of the widow."**

May they enact policies and initiatives that promote economic empowerment, equal opportunities, and social justice for all. Lord, we lift up to You the organizations and individuals who work tirelessly to combat poverty and its root causes. Your Word encourages us in **Galatians 6:9, "Let us not become weary in doing good, for at the proper time we will reap a harvest if we do not give up."** Strengthen their efforts, multiply their resources, and grant them wisdom and perseverance in their mission to bring hope and dignity to the impoverished.

Father, we pray for a transformation of hearts and minds, both in the privileged and the underprivileged, that we may see one another through Your eyes and extend compassion and solidarity to those in need.

Your Word teaches us in **James 2:14-17, "What good is it, my brothers and sisters, if someone claims to have faith but has no deeds? Can such faith save them? Suppose a brother or a sister is without clothes and daily food. If one**

Prayer for
Poverty

of you says to them, "Go in peace; keep warm and well fed," but does nothing about their physical needs, what good is it? In the same way, faith by itself, if it is not accompanied by action, is dead."

Lord, we commit the cause of ending poverty into Your hands, knowing that You are a God of justice and mercy. Your Word assures us in **Psalm 9:18, "But God will never forget the needy; the hope of the afflicted will never perish."** May Your kingdom of abundance and righteousness come, where every person is valued, empowered, and given the opportunity to flourish.

In Jesus' name, we pray,
Amen.

Prayer for Power

Heavenly Father,

I come before You humbly, acknowledging Your sovereignty and power over all things. Your word in **Ephesians 1:19-20** reminds me of the immeasurable greatness of Your power toward us who believe, according to the working of Your great might that You worked in Christ when You raised Him from the dead and seated Him at Your right hand in the heavenly places.

Lord, I ask for a fresh outpouring of Your power in my life today. Fill me with Your Holy Spirit, that I may be strengthened with power in my inner being, as mentioned in **Ephesians 3:16**. Grant me the courage to walk boldly in the authority You have given me as Your child.

Help me to recognize and utilize the gifts of power, love, and self-control that You have bestowed upon me, as stated in **2 Timothy 1:7**. May I not shrink back in fear or doubt, but instead, may I step forward with confidence, knowing that You are with me every step of the way.

Lord, I pray for Your power to be evident in my actions, my words, and my thoughts. May I be a vessel through which Your power flows, bringing light into the darkness and hope to the hopeless.

Thank You, Lord, for the promise of Your power in my life. May I rely on Your strength alone, knowing that nothing is impossible for You.

In Jesus' name, I pray,
Amen.

Prayer for Praising God

Heavenly Father,

I come before You today with a heart overflowing with praise and adoration for who You are. You are the Alpha and the Omega, the beginning and the end, the Creator of all things visible and invisible as written in **Revelation 22:13**. You are worthy of all honor, glory, and praise.

Lord, I praise You for Your infinite wisdom, for You are the source of all knowledge and understanding. Your ways are higher than our ways, and Your thoughts higher than our thoughts as mentioned in **Isaiah 55:9**. I marvel at the depth of Your wisdom displayed in creation and in the unfolding of history.

I praise You for Your boundless love and mercy, for You demonstrated Your love for us in this: while we were still sinners, Christ died for us. Your love knows no bounds, and Your mercy endures forever as written in **Psalm 136:1**. Thank You for the gift of salvation through Jesus Christ, our Savior and Redeemer.

Lord, I praise You for Your faithfulness and steadfastness. You are the same yesterday, today, and forever. Your promises are sure, and Your word never fails as reassured in **Isaiah 55:11**. Thank You for being a God who can be trusted and relied upon in every circumstance.

I praise You for Your goodness and grace, for You are the giver of every good and perfect gift as mentioned in **James 1:17**. Your blessings are abundant, and Your mercies are new every morning. Thank You for providing for all our needs according to Your riches in glory.

Lord, I praise You for Your sovereignty and power, for You are the King of kings and the Lord of lords. Nothing is impossible for You, and no purpose of Yours can be stopped as mentioned in **Job 42:2**. You are the Almighty God, who reigns over all the earth.

I praise You, Lord, with all my heart, soul, mind, and strength. May my life be a continual offering of praise and worship to You, both now and forevermore.

In Jesus' name, I pray,
Amen.

Prayer for
Pray for the Lost

Heavenly Father,

We come before You with heavy hearts, burdened for those who are lost and wandering without knowing You. Your word tells us in **Luke 19:10** that You came to seek and save the lost, and we lift up to You all those who are still searching for truth and salvation.

Lord Jesus, You are the way, the truth, and the life as written in **John 14:6**. We pray that You would reveal Yourself to those who are lost, opening their eyes to see the beauty of Your grace and the depth of Your love for them. Help them to understand that You are the only path to true fulfillment and eternal life.

Father, we ask that You would send laborers into the harvest fields, as You commanded in **Matthew 9:38**. Raise up bold witnesses who will proclaim Your gospel with clarity and conviction, leading the lost into a personal relationship with You.

We pray for divine appointments and opportunities to share the good news of salvation with those who are still in darkness. Give us the words to speak and the wisdom to guide them gently into Your loving embrace.

Lord, Your heart longs for all to come to repentance as written in **2 Peter 3:9**, and we join with You in that desire. Pour out Your Spirit upon the lost, convicting them of sin, righteousness, and judgment, and drawing them into a saving knowledge of Jesus Christ.

Father, we also pray for perseverance and patience as we intercede for the lost. Help us to trust in Your perfect timing and to never lose hope in Your power to save.

May Your kingdom come and Your will be done in the lives of those who are lost, as it is in heaven. We commit them into Your hands, knowing that You are able to save completely those who come to You as mentioned in **Hebrews 7:25**.

In Jesus' name, we pray,
Amen.

Prayer for Prisoners

Heavenly Father,

I lift up to You all those who are currently incarcerated, knowing that Your love and grace extend to every person, regardless of their circumstances. Your word reminds us in **Matthew 25:36** that when we visit those in prison, we are ministering to You. So, Lord, I come before You on behalf of these individuals, asking for Your mercy and compassion to surround them.

Father, we pray for their physical safety and well-being while they are in prison. Protect them from harm and grant them strength to endure the challenges they face each day. Help them to find hope and peace in the midst of their confinement.

We also lift up their spiritual needs to You, Lord. Your word in **Psalm 34:18** assures us that You are near to the brokenhearted and save the crushed in spirit. We ask that You draw near to those who are feeling lost, lonely, or broken-hearted in prison. Bring comfort to their souls and reveal Your love and forgiveness to them in a powerful way.

Lord, we pray for transformation in their lives. Your word in **2 Corinthians 5:17** tells us that anyone who is in Christ is a new creation; the old has passed away, and the new has come. We ask that You work in the hearts of those who are incarcerated, bringing about genuine repentance, redemption, and renewal. Let Your light shine in the darkness of their circumstances, bringing hope and healing to their lives.

Father, we also pray for their families and loved ones who are affected by their incarceration. Comfort them in their times of worry and uncertainty, and help them to remain steadfast in their faith and love for You.

May Your grace abound in the lives of all those who are in prison, Lord, bringing about reconciliation, restoration, and healing. Use this time of confinement to draw them closer to You and to reveal Your purposes for their lives.

In Jesus' name, we pray,
Amen.

Prayer for
Prosperity

Heavenly Father,

We come before You today with hearts full of gratitude for the abundant blessings You have bestowed upon us. Your word tells us in **Malachi 3:10, "Bring the whole tithe into the storehouse, that there may be food in my house. Test me in this," says the Lord Almighty, "and see if I will not throw open the floodgates of heaven and pour out so much blessing that there will not be room enough to store it."** We trust in Your promise, Lord, and we commit to honoring You with our tithes and offerings.

Lord, we pray for prosperity in all areas of our lives—financial, emotional, spiritual, and relational. You have promised to prosper us and not to harm us, to give us hope and a future as written in **Jeremiah 29:11**. We claim this promise over our lives today.

We ask for wisdom and discernment in managing our finances, Lord. Help us to be good stewards of the resources You have entrusted to us, using them wisely for Your kingdom purposes.

We pray for abundance in our work and businesses, Lord. Your word tells us in **Deuteronomy 8:18, "But remember the Lord your God, for it is he who gives you the ability to produce wealth, and so confirms his covenant, which he swore to your ancestors, as it is today."** May our endeavors be blessed and prosperous, bringing glory to Your name.

Lord, we also pray for prosperity in our relationships and our health. May we experience wholeness and abundance in every area of our lives, knowing that You are our provider and sustainer.

We surrender our desires for prosperity into Your hands, trusting in Your perfect timing and Your unfailing love. May Your will be done in our lives, and may we always seek first Your kingdom and Your righteousness, knowing that all these things will be added unto us, as You clearly mentioned in **Matthew 6:33**.

In Jesus' name we pray,
Amen.

Prayer for
Protection over Marriage

Heavenly Father,

I come before You today, lifting up my marriage before Your throne of grace. Your word tells us in **Ecclesiastes 4:12, "Though one may be overpowered, two can defend themselves. A cord of three strands is not quickly broken."** Lord, I ask that You be the third strand in our marriage, binding us together with Your love and strength.

Father, I pray for Your divine protection over our marriage. Shield us from the attacks of the enemy and guard us against any schemes designed to divide us. Your word assures us in **Psalm 91:10-11, "No harm will overtake you, no disaster will come near your tent. For he will command his angels concerning you to guard you in all your ways."** May Your angels surround us and watch over our union, preserving it from harm.

Lord, I pray for unity and harmony in our marriage. Help us to communicate with love and understanding, to forgive one another as You have forgiven us, and to prioritize our relationship above all else. Your word reminds us in **Colossians 3:14, "And over all these virtues put on love, which binds them all together in perfect unity."** May Your love bind us together as one, strengthening the bonds of our marriage.

Father, I pray for wisdom and discernment for both of us as we navigate the joys and challenges of married life. Your word instructs us in **Proverbs 3:5-6, "Trust in the Lord with all your heart and lean not on your own understanding; in all your ways submit to him, and he will make your paths straight."** Guide us in our decisions and help us to submit to Your will in all things.

Lord, I surrender our marriage into Your hands, trusting in Your faithfulness to guide and protect us. Your word assures us in **Psalm 32:8, "I will instruct you and teach you in the way you should go; I will counsel you with my loving eye on you."** May we always look to You for guidance and direction, knowing that You are with us every step of the way.

In Jesus' name, I pray,
Amen.

Prayer for
Purity

Heavenly Father,

I come before You with a humble heart, acknowledging my need for purity in every aspect of my life. Your Word teaches us in **Psalm 51:10, "Create in me a pure heart, O God, and renew a steadfast spirit within me."**

Lord, I confess any impurity in my thoughts, words, and actions. I repent of any sinful behaviors or attitudes that have tainted my heart and soul. Wash me clean, O God, and purify me from within by the power of Your Holy Spirit.

Your Word instructs us in **1 Thessalonians 4:3-4, "It is God's will that you should be sanctified: that you should avoid sexual immorality; that each of you should learn to control your own body in a way that is holy and honorable."** Help me, Lord, to live a life of purity and holiness, honoring You in all that I do.

I pray for purity of mind, that my thoughts may be free from lust, envy, and impurity. Your Word in **Philippians 4:8** encourages us to think about "whatever is true, whatever is noble, whatever is right, whatever is pure, whatever is lovely, whatever is admirable." May my mind be filled with thoughts that honor and glorify You.

I pray for purity of speech, that my words may be uplifting and edifying to others. Your Word in **Ephesians 4:29** cautions us, **"Do not let any unwholesome talk come out of your mouths, but only what is helpful for building others up according to their needs, that it may benefit those who listen."** Help me to speak words of kindness, encouragement, and truth.

I pray for purity of heart, that my desires may be aligned with Yours. Your Word in **Matthew 5:8** declares, **"Blessed are the pure in heart, for they will see God."** Purify my heart, O Lord, and help me to seek after You with sincerity and devotion.

I surrender my life to You, Lord, asking for Your grace and strength to walk in purity each day. Fill me afresh with Your Holy Spirit, that I may live a life that is pleasing to You and brings glory to Your name.

In Jesus' name, I pray,
Amen.

Prayer for Racism

Heavenly Father,

We come before You humbly, acknowledging the sin of racism that plagues our world and grieves Your heart. Your Word teaches us in **Galatians 3:28, "There is neither Jew nor Gentile, neither slave nor free, nor is there male and female, for you are all one in Christ Jesus."** Yet, we recognize that racism continues to divide and oppress Your children, creating barriers to unity, understanding, and love.

Lord Jesus, You who embraced all people regardless of their race or background, help us to follow Your example and love one another deeply. Your Word instructs us in **John 13:34-35, "A new command I give you: Love one another. As I have loved you, so you must love one another. By this everyone will know that you are my disciples, if you love one another."** Grant us the grace to see each person as Your beloved creation, worthy of dignity, respect, and equality.

Father, we repent of the ways in which we have perpetuated or remained silent in the face of racism. Your Word admonishes us in **James 2:9, "But if you show favoritism, you sin and are convicted by the law as lawbreakers."** Forgive us for the times when we have failed to speak out against injustice or have harbored prejudice in our hearts. Create in us clean hearts and renew a right spirit within us.

Lord, we pray for healing and reconciliation in our communities and nations. Your Word promises in **2 Chronicles 7:14, "if my people, who are called by my name, will humble themselves and pray and seek my face and turn from their wicked ways, then I will hear from heaven, and I will forgive their sin and will heal their land."** May we humble ourselves before You, seeking Your face and turning from the sin of racism. Bring healing to the wounds caused by prejudice and discrimination and unite us in Your love.

Father, we lift up to You those who have been marginalized, oppressed, and victimized because of their race. Your Word assures us in **Psalm 9:9, "The Lord is a refuge for the oppressed, a stronghold in times of trouble."** Comfort them in their pain, strengthen them in their resilience, and empower them to stand firm in their identity as Your cherished children.

Prayer for Racism

Lord, we pray for wisdom and courage for our leaders, policymakers, and authorities as they work to dismantle systems of racism and promote justice and equality. Your Word guides us in **Micah 6:8, "And what does the Lord require of you? To act justly and to love mercy and to walk humbly with your God."**

Grant them discernment and integrity in their efforts to bring about positive change.

Father, may Your Church rise up as a beacon of hope and reconciliation in a divided world. Your Word exhorts us in **Ephesians 4:3, "Make every effort to keep the unity of the Spirit through the bond of peace."** May we actively pursue unity and reconciliation, modeling Your love and grace to all people, regardless of their race or ethnicity.

Lord, we commit the fight against racism into Your hands, trusting in Your power to bring about transformation and renewal. Your Word proclaims in **Revelation 7:9, "After this I looked, and there before me was a great multitude that no one could count, from every nation, tribe, people and language, standing before the throne and before the Lamb. They were wearing white robes and were holding palm branches in their hands."** May Your kingdom of diversity and unity be realized on earth as it is in heaven.

In Jesus' name, we pray,
Amen.

Prayer for
Rebuking curses in our lives

Heavenly Father,

In the name of Jesus Christ, we come before You to rebuke any curses that may have been spoken over our lives or the lives of those around us. Your Word tells us in **Genesis 12:3, "I will bless those who bless you, and whoever curses you I will curse; and all peoples on earth will be blessed through you."**

Lord, we trust in Your power and authority to break every curse that is not in alignment with Your will. Your Word also assures us in **Galatians 3:13-14, "Christ redeemed us from the curse of the law by becoming a curse for us, for it is written: 'Cursed is everyone who is hung on a pole.'** He redeemed us in order that the blessing given to Abraham might come to the Gentiles through Christ Jesus, so that by faith we might receive the promise of the Spirit."

In the name of Jesus, we declare that every curse spoken against us is null and void. We break its power and influence over our lives, for we are redeemed by the blood of Jesus Christ.

Lord, we pray for forgiveness for any sins or transgressions that may have opened the door to curses in our lives. We ask for Your cleansing and purification, washing away every stain of sin by the blood of Jesus.

We declare Your promises of blessing and protection over our lives, for Your Word tells us in **Romans 8:37-39, "in all these things we are more than conquerors through him who loved us. For I am convinced that neither death nor life, neither angels nor demons, neither the present nor the future, nor any powers, neither height nor depth, nor anything else in all creation, will be able to separate us from the love of God that is in Christ Jesus our Lord."**

We thank You, Lord, for Your faithfulness and Your promise to bless us and keep us safe from harm. Help us to walk in obedience to Your Word, trusting in Your unfailing love and protection.

In Jesus' name we pray,
Amen.

Prayer for
Rebuking evil spirits

Heavenly Father,

In the name of Jesus Christ, we come before You to rebuke any evil spirits that may be at work in our lives or the lives of those around us. Your Word tells us in **James 4:7, "Submit yourselves, then, to God. Resist the devil, and he will flee from you."**

Lord, we submit ourselves to You, recognizing Your authority and power over all evil. We stand firm in our faith, knowing that You have given us authority over every demonic force and spiritual darkness. As it says in **Luke 10:19, "I have given you authority to trample on snakes and scorpions and to overcome all the power of the enemy; nothing will harm you."**

In the mighty name of Jesus, we rebuke every evil spirit that seeks to bring harm, destruction, or oppression into our lives. We command them to flee from us and to have no power over us, for greater is He who is in us than he who is in the world as declared in **1 John 4:4**.

Lord, we ask that You would fill us with Your Holy Spirit, empowering us to stand strong against the schemes of the enemy. Clothe us with the armor of God, as described in **Ephesians 6:10-18**, so that we may be able to withstand the attacks of the devil.

We pray for protection over our minds, hearts, and spirits, that we may be guarded against the lies and deceptions of the evil one. Let Your light shine in the darkness, Lord, and expose every hidden work of darkness.

We declare victory in Jesus' name, knowing that nothing can separate us from Your love and that You have already won the ultimate victory over sin, death, and the devil through the death and resurrection of Your Son, Jesus Christ.

In Jesus' name we pray,
Amen.

Prayer for Receiving Prophetic Words and Revelations

Heavenly Father,

We come before You in reverence and awe, recognizing Your sovereignty over all things and Your ability to reveal Your will to us through prophecy and revelation. Your Word declares in **Amos 3:7, "Surely the Sovereign Lord does nothing without revealing his plan to his servants the prophets."** We thank You for the gift of prophecy and the revelations You provide to guide and instruct Your people.

Lord, we ask for open hearts and minds to receive Your prophetic word and revelations. Your Word teaches us in **1 Thessalonians 5:20-21, "Do not treat prophecies with contempt but test them all; hold on to what is good."** Help us to discern Your voice amidst the noise of the world and to hold fast to the truth revealed through Your prophets.

Grant us, O Lord, the wisdom and discernment to interpret and apply Your prophetic messages in accordance with Your will. Your Word instructs us in **2 Peter 1:20-21, "Above all, you must understand that no prophecy of Scripture came about by the prophet's own interpretation of things. For prophecy never had its origin in the human will, but prophets, though human, spoke from God as they were carried along by the Holy Spirit."** May we rely on the guidance of Your Holy Spirit to understand and obey Your prophetic word.

Father, we pray for Your prophets and messengers whom You have chosen to speak Your word to Your people. Protect them from deception and persecution and strengthen them to boldly proclaim Your truth. Your Word assures us in **Jeremiah 1:9-10, "Then the Lord reached out his hand and touched my mouth and said to me, 'I have put my words in your mouth. See, today I appoint you over nations and kingdoms to uproot and tear down, to destroy and overthrow, to build and to plant.'"** May Your prophets be faithful stewards of the messages You have entrusted to them, proclaiming Your word with boldness and clarity.

Lord, we pray for a spirit of humility and reverence as we seek Your prophetic guidance. Your Word reminds us in **Revelation 19:10, "For it is the Spirit of prophecy who bears testimony to Jesus."** May all prophecy and revelation ultimately point us to Jesus Christ, the living Word, and deepen our relationship with Him.

In Jesus' name, we pray,
Amen.

Prayer for Rejection

Heavenly Father,

I come before You with a heavy heart, feeling the pain of rejection weighing upon me. Your Word in **Psalm 34:18**, tells me that You are close to the brokenhearted and save those who are crushed in spirit. Lord, I need Your comfort and strength in this time of hurt.

Father, I confess that rejection has wounded me deeply, causing me to doubt my worth and value. But Your Word in **Psalm 139:14** reminds me that I am fearfully and wonderfully made in Your image, and that You have chosen me and called me by name as written in **Isaiah 43:1**. Help me to find my identity and security in You alone.

Lord, when I am rejected by others, help me to remember that You will never leave me nor forsake me as written in **Hebrews 13:5**. Your love for me is unconditional and everlasting, and nothing can separate me from Your love as promised in **Romans 8:38-39**. Strengthen me with the assurance of Your presence and Your acceptance.

Father, I pray for healing from the wounds of rejection. Pour out Your healing balm upon my heart and soul and restore to me the joy of Your salvation as written in **Psalm 51:12**. Help me to forgive those who have hurt me and to release the pain and bitterness that I carry.

Lord, I surrender my need for acceptance to You. Help me to find my fulfillment and satisfaction in You alone, knowing that You are enough for me. Teach me to trust in Your perfect plan for my life, even when others reject or misunderstand me.

Father, I pray for the grace to extend love and kindness to those who reject me, following the example of Jesus who prayed in **Luke 23:34, "Father, forgive them, for they do not know what they are doing"**. Help me to reflect Your love and grace to others, even in the face of rejection.

Lord, I thank You for Your faithfulness and Your unconditional love. Help me to cling to Your promises and to find my security in You alone. May Your peace, which surpasses all understanding, guard my heart and mind in Christ Jesus as mentioned in **Philippians 4:7**.

In Jesus' name, I pray,
Amen.

Prayer for Relatives

Heavenly Father,

We come before You with gratitude for the gift of family and the blessing of relatives. Your Word teaches us in **Psalm 133:1, "How good and pleasant it is when God's people live together in unity!"** We thank You for the bond of love that unites us as relatives and for the support and encouragement we find in one another.

Lord, we lift up our relatives to You, knowing that each one is precious in Your sight. Your Word assures us in **Psalm 139:13-14, "For you created my inmost being; you knit me together in my mother's womb. I praise you because I am fearfully and wonderfully made; your works are wonderful, I know that full well."** Help us to honor and cherish each relative as a unique creation of Yours, deserving of love and respect.

Father, we pray for unity and harmony among our relatives. Your Word instructs us in **Ephesians 4:3, "Make every effort to keep the unity of the Spirit through the bond of peace."** May we strive to maintain peace and reconciliation in our relationships, seeking forgiveness and extending grace to one another.

Lord, we ask for Your blessing upon each member of our extended family. Your Word promises in **Psalm 67:1-2, "May God be gracious to us and bless us and make his face shine on us—so that your ways may be known on earth, your salvation among all nations."** May Your grace and favor rest upon our relatives, guiding them in Your ways and showering them with Your blessings.

Father, we pray for the spiritual well-being of our relatives. Your Word encourages us in **3 John 1:4, "I have no greater joy than to hear that my children are walking in the truth."** May each relative come to know You personally and walk faithfully in Your ways, experiencing the joy and peace that come from a relationship with You.

Lord, we lift up any specific needs or concerns within our family. Your Word assures us in **Philippians 4:6-7, "Do not be anxious about anything, but in every situation, by prayer and petition, with thanksgiving, present your requests to God. And the peace of God, which transcends all understanding, will guard your hearts and your minds in Christ Jesus."** May Your peace reign in the hearts of our relatives, and may You provide for every need according to Your riches in glory.

Father, we commit our relatives into Your loving hands, trusting in Your faithfulness to watch over them and to guide them in all their ways. May our family be a testimony to Your love and grace, shining brightly for Your glory.

In Jesus' name, we pray,
Amen.

Prayer for Renewal of Mind

Heavenly Father,

I come before You with a heart open to Your transformative power, recognizing the need for the renewal of my mind. Your Word in **Romans 12:2** instructs us, **"Do not conform to the pattern of this world, but be transformed by the renewing of your mind. Then you will be able to test and approve what God's will is—his good, pleasing and perfect will."**

Lord, I confess that there are areas of my mind that need to be renewed according to Your truth. Forgive me for allowing worldly influences, negative thoughts, and harmful beliefs to shape my thinking. I surrender my mind to You, asking for Your Holy Spirit to bring about a transformation from within.

I pray for the washing of Your Word to cleanse my mind of any falsehoods or misconceptions. Your Word in **Ephesians 4:23-24** encourages us to **"be made new in the attitude of your minds; and to put on the new self, created to be like God in true righteousness and holiness."** May my mind be renewed to align with Your truth and righteousness.

Help me, Lord, to think thoughts that are pleasing to You and in accordance with Your Word. Your Word in **Philippians 4:8** instructs us, **"Finally, brothers and sisters, whatever is true, whatever is noble, whatever is right, whatever is pure, whatever is lovely, whatever is admirable—if anything is excellent or praiseworthy—think about such things."** May my mind be filled with thoughts that honor and glorify You.

I pray for discernment to recognize and reject any lies or deceptions that the enemy may try to plant in my mind. Your Word in **2 Corinthians 10:5** teaches us to **"take captive every thought to make it obedient to Christ."** Help me to guard my mind diligently and to take captive any thought that is not in line with Your truth.

Lord, I invite You to renew my mind daily through the power of Your Word and the work of Your Spirit within me. May my mind be transformed to reflect the mind of Christ, and may I experience the freedom and peace that come from thinking in alignment with Your truth. I surrender my thoughts, beliefs, and attitudes to You, Lord, trusting in Your faithfulness to renew my mind and lead me in the path of righteousness.

In Jesus' name, I pray,
Amen.

Prayer for Responsibility

Heavenly Father,

I come before You acknowledging the responsibility You have entrusted to me in various aspects of my life. Your Word teaches us in **Luke 12:48, "From everyone who has been given much, much will be demanded; and from the one who has been entrusted with much, much more will be asked."**

Lord, I recognize the weight of responsibility placed upon my shoulders, and I ask for Your guidance and strength to fulfill it faithfully. Help me to steward well the gifts, talents, and resources You have given me, whether in my family, work, community, or ministry.

Your Word instructs us in **Proverbs 16:3, "Commit to the Lord whatever you do, and he will establish your plans."** I commit my responsibilities to You, Lord, trusting in Your wisdom and guidance to direct my steps and establish my plans according to Your will.

I pray for wisdom to make sound decisions and discernment to prioritize my responsibilities according to Your purposes. Your Word in **James 1:5** assures us, **"If any of you lacks wisdom, you should ask God, who gives generously to all without finding fault, and it will be given to you."** Grant me wisdom, O Lord, as I navigate the challenges and choices before me.

I pray for diligence and perseverance to carry out my responsibilities with excellence and integrity. Your Word in **Colossians 3:23-24** reminds us, **"Whatever you do, work at it with all your heart, as working for the Lord, not for human masters, since you know that you will receive an inheritance from the Lord as a reward. It is the Lord Christ you are serving."** Help me to work diligently and wholeheartedly, knowing that I am serving You, Lord.

I pray for humility to recognize that apart from You, I can do nothing. Your Word in **Philippians 4:13** declares, **"I can do all this through him who gives me strength."** May I rely on Your strength and grace to fulfill my responsibilities according to Your purposes and for Your glory. Thank You, Lord, for the privilege and opportunity to serve You through the responsibilities You have entrusted to me. May my life be a reflection of Your love, grace, and faithfulness as I seek to honor You in all that I do.

In Jesus' name, I pray,
Amen.

Prayer for **Restoration**

Heavenly Father,

We come before You with hearts full of hope and faith, trusting in Your promise of restoration for those who seek You. Your Word assures us that You are the God of restoration, who can renew and revive that which has been broken and lost.

Lord, we acknowledge our need for restoration in our lives. We confess our sins, failures, and shortcomings before You, knowing that You are faithful and just to forgive us and to cleanse us from all unrighteousness as written in **1 John 1:9**. We ask for Your forgiveness and mercy, believing that You are able to restore us to a right relationship with You.

Father, we pray for restoration in our relationships. Heal brokenness, mend wounds, and reconcile estranged hearts. Help us to forgive one another as You have forgiven us, and to love one another with the same love with which You have loved us as You taught us in **Ephesians 4:32**.

Lord Jesus, You are the great Restorer of all things. You have promised in **Isaiah 61:3** to make all things new and to bring beauty out of ashes. We pray for restoration in our homes, our families, our communities, and our nation. Bring healing where there is sickness, peace where there is conflict, and hope where there is despair.

Holy Spirit, we invite You to come and move in our midst, bringing restoration and renewal to every area of our lives. Fill us with Your presence and power, empowering us to walk in obedience to Your will and to experience the fullness of Your restoration in our lives.

Lord, we thank You for Your faithfulness and love. We trust in Your promise to restore us and to make us whole. May Your name be glorified through the restoration work You do in us and through us.

In Jesus' name, we pray,
Amen.

Prayer for
Revival

Heavenly Father,

We come before You with hearts full of longing for revival, both in our own lives and in the world around us. Your word tells us in **2 Chronicles 7:14** that if Your people, who are called by Your name, humble themselves, pray, seek Your face, and turn from their wicked ways, then You will hear from heaven, forgive their sin, and heal their land.

Lord, we acknowledge our need for revival. We humble ourselves before You, recognizing our dependence on Your grace and mercy. We pray, seeking Your face, desiring to know You more deeply and intimately. Help us to turn away from all sin and disobedience, and to turn wholeheartedly to You.

Father, we pray for a revival of passion for Your word and Your truth. Your word is living and active, sharper than any two-edged sword, piercing to the division of soul and spirit, of joints and of marrow, and discerning the thoughts and intentions of the heart as written in **Hebrews 4:12**. May Your word penetrate our hearts and minds, transforming us from the inside out.

Lord, we pray for a revival of love for one another within Your church. Your word tells us in **John 13:35** that all people will know that we are Your disciples if we have love for one another. May our love for one another be a powerful testimony to the world of Your love and grace.

Father, we pray for a revival of evangelism and mission, that Your gospel may be proclaimed to the ends of the earth. Your word in **Matthew 28:19-20** commands us to go and make disciples of all nations, baptizing them in the name of the Father, and of the Son, and of the Holy Spirit, and teaching them to obey everything You have commanded us. Grant us boldness and courage to share the good news of Jesus Christ with those who are lost and in need of salvation.

Lord, we pray for a revival of holiness and righteousness in our lives and in Your church. Your Word in **1 Peter 1:16** calls us to be holy as You are holy, and to pursue righteousness, godliness, faith, love, steadfastness, and gentleness as written in **1 Timothy 6:11**. May Your Spirit empower us to live lives that are pleasing to You in every way.

Prayer for
Revival

Father, we pray for a revival of prayer, both individually and corporately. Your word tells us in **James 5:16** that the prayer of a righteous person is powerful and effective. May we be fervent and persistent in prayer, seeking Your will and Your kingdom above all else.

Lord, we pray for a revival of Your presence and power in our midst. Your Word in **Matthew 18:20** assures us that where two or three are gathered in Your name, You are there among them, and that Your Spirit will be poured out on all flesh as written in **Joel 2:28**.

May we experience a fresh outpouring of Your Spirit, filling us with Your love, joy, peace, patience, kindness, goodness, faithfulness, gentleness, and self-control as written in **Galatians 5:22-23**.

Father, we thank You for Your faithfulness and Your promise to hear and answer our prayers. We trust in Your timing and Your sovereign plan for revival, and we eagerly await the day when Your kingdom will come and Your will will be done on earth as it is in heaven.

In Jesus' name, we pray,
Amen.

Prayer for
Salvation for the Unsaved

Heavenly Father,

I come before You with a heavy heart, knowing that there are still many who have not experienced the life-transforming love of Your Son, Jesus Christ. I lift up **[Name]**, who has not yet come to know Jesus as their Savior. Lord, You desire that none should perish but that all should come to repentance as written in **2 Peter 3:9**. I pray earnestly for **[Name]**'s salvation, that they may experience the joy and freedom found in knowing You.

Father, Your Word tells us in **John 14:6** that Jesus is the way, the truth, and the life, and no one comes to the Father except through Him. I pray that You would open **[Name]**'s eyes to see the truth of who Jesus is, that they may come to understand and accept Him as their Lord and Savior.

Lord, I ask that You would send laborers into **[Name]**'s life, as Jesus instructed us in **Matthew 9:38**, to share the Gospel with them in a way that they can understand and receive. Soften **[Name]**'s heart to receive Your word, and remove any obstacles or barriers that may be hindering them from accepting Jesus into their life.

Father, I pray that You would reveal Your love and grace to **[Name]** in a powerful way, drawing them to Yourself and leading them into a personal relationship with Jesus. Give them a hunger and thirst for righteousness, and fill them with a desire to seek You with all their heart.

Lord, I commit **[Name]**'s salvation into Your hands, trusting in Your perfect timing and sovereignty. May Your Holy Spirit continue to work in **[Name]**'s life, convicting them of sin, righteousness, and judgment, and drawing them into a saving knowledge of Jesus Christ.

Thank You, Lord, for Your faithfulness and Your desire to save the lost. May **[Name]** come to know the joy and peace that can only be found in Jesus.

In His name, I pray,
Amen.

Prayer for
Saying Grace before a meal

Heavenly Father,

As we gather around this table to partake of the food You have graciously provided, we pause to give You thanks and praise for Your abundant provision. Your word declares in **Psalm 136:1, "Give thanks to the Lord, for he is good; his love endures forever."** We are grateful for Your faithfulness and generosity, which sustain us each day.

Lord, as written in **James 1:17**, we acknowledge that every good gift comes from You, and we thank You for the nourishment before us. Bless this food to our bodies and strengthen us physically, mentally, and spiritually as we partake of it. May it fuel us for the tasks ahead and enable us to serve You and others with joy and vigor.

As we enjoy this meal together, may our fellowship be sweet and our conversation uplifting. Help us to be mindful of those who are less fortunate and to share generously with those in need. Your word instructs us in **Luke 3:11, "Anyone who has two shirts should share with the one who has none, and anyone who has food should do the same."** May we always be mindful of our responsibility to care for others.

Lord, we also remember those who are hungry and in need around the world. May Your provision reach them swiftly, and may they experience Your love and compassion through the hands and hearts of those who serve them.

In all things, Lord, may Your name be glorified. We give You thanks for this meal, for the hands that prepared it, and for the fellowship we share. May our hearts overflow with gratitude and praise to You, now and forevermore.

In Jesus' name, we pray,
Amen.

Prayer for
School and Education

Heavenly Father,

I come before You today with thanksgiving in my heart for the opportunity to pursue education, knowing that every good gift comes from You as mentioned in **James 1:17**. I acknowledge that You are the source of all knowledge and wisdom, and I ask for Your guidance and direction in my studies.

Lord, Your Word tells us in **Proverbs 2:6, "For the Lord gives wisdom; from his mouth come knowledge and understanding."** I pray that You would grant me wisdom and understanding as I engage in learning, that I may grasp the concepts and ideas presented before me.

I also lift up my teachers, professors, and instructors to You, Lord. May they be filled with Your wisdom and knowledge as they impart their expertise to me. Help me to honor and respect them, recognizing the role they play in my education.

Father, I pray for diligence and perseverance in my studies. Your Word encourages us in **Colossians 3:23, "Whatever you do, work at it with all your heart, as working for the Lord, not for human masters."**

Lord, may I approach my studies with dedication and commitment, striving for excellence in all that I do.

I ask for Your peace to guard my mind and heart amidst the challenges and pressures of academic life. Your Word assures us in **Philippians 4:6-7, "Do not be anxious about anything, but in every situation, by prayer and petition, with thanksgiving, present your requests to God. And the peace of God, which transcends all understanding, will guard your hearts and your minds in Christ Jesus."**

Lord, I commit my education into Your hands, trusting in Your plan and purpose for my life. May my studies be a means of glorifying You and serving others. Lead me in the paths of righteousness, and may I walk in obedience to Your will.

In Jesus' name I pray,
Amen.

Prayer for Self Control

Heavenly Father,

I come before You today with a humble heart, acknowledging my need for self-control in all areas of my life. Your Word teaches us in **Galatians 5:22-23** that self-control is a fruit of the Spirit, and I pray that You would cultivate this fruit within me.

Lord, Your Word also tells us in **Proverbs 16:32, "Better a patient person than a warrior, one with self-control than one who takes a city."** Help me to guard my heart and mind with the strength of Your Spirit, that I may resist temptation and walk in obedience to Your will.

Father, You have promised in **1 Corinthians 10:13** that You will not allow us to be tempted beyond what we can bear, but with the temptation, You will also provide a way of escape. Give me the wisdom to recognize the way of escape when temptation comes, and the courage to take it.

Teach me to discipline my thoughts, my words, and my actions according to Your Word. Help me to be diligent in prayer and in seeking Your guidance, that I may be led by Your Spirit and not by my flesh.

Lord, I surrender my desires and weaknesses to You, knowing that in my weakness, Your strength is made perfect. Fill me with Your Spirit, that I may bear fruit worthy of repentance and bring glory to Your name.

Grant me the grace to exercise self-control in all things, whether it be in my relationships, my finances, my habits, or my desires. Help me to fix my eyes on Jesus, the author and perfecter of my faith, who endured the cross for the joy set before him.

In every moment of weakness, may I find strength in You, knowing that You are faithful to uphold me and empower me to overcome. Thank You, Lord, for the gift of self-control and for the victory that is mine through Christ Jesus.

In His name, I pray,
Amen.

Prayer for
Self Respect and Self Esteem

Heavenly Father,

I come before You with a heart full of gratitude for the unique identity and worth You have bestowed upon me as Your creation. Your Word teaches me in **Psalm 139:14** that I am fearfully and wonderfully made, and I praise You for the beauty of Your craftsmanship.

Lord, I confess that there are times when I struggle with feelings of inadequacy and low self-esteem. In those moments, help me to remember the truth of Your Word, which tells me in **Ephesians 2:10** that I am Your workmanship, created in Christ Jesus for good works, which You prepared beforehand, that I should walk in them.

Father, I pray that You would strengthen my sense of self-respect and self-worth, not based on the opinions of others or the standards of this world, but rooted in the knowledge of who I am in Christ. Remind me that I am loved unconditionally by You, as stated in **Romans 5:8**, that while I was still a sinner, Christ died for me.

Help me to see myself through Your eyes, as a beloved child of God, redeemed and forgiven through the blood of Jesus Christ. Fill me with the confidence and assurance that comes from knowing that I am accepted and valued by You.

Lord, guard my heart and mind from negative self-talk and comparisons with others. Instead, help me to focus on the truth of Your Word, which tells me in **Philippians 4:8** to think about whatever is true, noble, right, pure, lovely and admirable.

Teach me to find my identity and worth in You alone, and not in the fleeting approval of this world. Help me to embrace the unique gifts, talents, and abilities You have given me, and to use them for Your glory and the benefit of others.

Thank You, Lord, for the immeasurable value You have placed upon me as Your child. May I live each day with confidence, knowing that I am loved, accepted, and cherished by You.

In Jesus' name, I pray,
Amen.

Prayer for Servant's Heart

Heavenly Father,

I come before You humbly, acknowledging that You are the ultimate example of a servant's heart. Your Word teaches us in **Philippians 2:5-7** that Jesus Christ, though He was in the form of God, He made Himself nothing, taking the form of a servant. I pray that You would mold my heart to be like His, filled with humility and a desire to serve others.

Lord, forgive me for the times when I have been selfish and prideful, seeking my own interests above those of others. Help me to follow the example of Jesus, who came not to be served, but to serve as written in **Matthew 20:28**. Teach me. O Lord as stated in **Philippians 2:3-4** to consider others as more significant than myself, looking not only to my own interests but also to the interests of others

Father, give me eyes to see the needs of those around me and a heart that is willing to meet those needs with love and compassion. Help me to serve others joyfully, knowing that in doing so, I am serving You as we are taught in **Colossians 3:23-24**. May my actions be motivated by love, reflecting Your love for me and for all humanity.

Lord, I pray for opportunities to serve in ways that honor You and build up Your kingdom. Open doors for me to use my gifts and talents to bless others and to make a positive impact in their lives. Help me to be faithful in the little things, knowing that You can use even the smallest acts of service for Your glory.

Father, I thank You for the privilege of serving You and others. May my life be a living testimony to Your love and grace, and may I always be willing to follow wherever You lead, with a servant's heart.

In Jesus' name, I pray,
Amen.

Prayer for Siblings

Heavenly Father,

I come before You today with a heart full of gratitude for the gift of my siblings *[NAMES]*. Thank You for the bond of love and friendship that we share, and for the unique ways in which each of them enriches my life. As it is written in **Ecclesiastes 4:9-10, "Two are better than one, because they have a good return for their labor: If either of them falls down, one can help the other up. But pity anyone who falls and has no one to help them up."**

Lord, I lift up my siblings to You now, knowing that You love them even more deeply than I ever could. I pray for their health, safety, and well-being, both physically and spiritually. Surround them with Your protection and guidance, and may they always feel Your presence by their side. As it is written in **Psalm 91:11-12, "For he will command his angels concerning you to guard you in all your ways; they will lift you up in their hands, so that you will not strike your foot against a stone."**

Father, I also pray for their growth and maturity, both in their relationships with You and with others. Grant them wisdom, discernment, and understanding as they navigate the challenges and opportunities of life. Help them to walk in integrity and righteousness, honoring You in all that they do. As it is written in **Proverbs 3:5-6, "Trust in the Lord with all your heart and lean not on your own understanding; in all your ways submit to him, and he will make your paths straight."**

Lord, I ask for unity and harmony among us as siblings. May we always support and encourage one another, celebrating each other's successes and offering comfort and strength in times of need. Help us to be a source of love and encouragement for one another, reflecting Your love to the world. As it is written in **1 Thessalonians 5:11, "Therefore encourage one another and build each other up, just as in fact you are doing."**

I commit my siblings into Your loving care, knowing that You have a plan and purpose for each of their lives. Guide them in their decisions, protect them from harm, and lead them along paths of righteousness for Your name's sake. May our bond as siblings continue to grow stronger with each passing day, and may we always be a blessing to one another and to those around us.

In Jesus' name I pray,
Amen.

Prayer for
Sick

Heavenly Father,

We come before You with heavy hearts, lifting up those who are sick and suffering. Your word tells us in **James 5:14-15, "Is anyone among you sick? Let them call the elders of the church to pray over them and anoint them with oil in the name of the Lord. And the prayer offered in faith will make the sick person well; the Lord will raise them up. If they have sinned, they will be forgiven."**

Lord, we ask for Your healing touch to be upon those who are sick and in need of Your divine intervention. We pray for physical healing, knowing that You are the Great Physician who can bring restoration and wholeness to our bodies. May Your healing power flow through them, bringing relief from pain, strength to weary limbs, and restoration to every part of their being.

Father, we also pray for emotional and spiritual healing for those who are suffering. Comfort them in their distress, Lord, and surround them with Your peace that surpasses all understanding. Bring healing to their hearts and minds and restore them to a place of joy and hope in You.

We lift up those who are caring for the sick, Lord. Give them strength, patience, and compassion as they minister to the needs of others. May they be a source of comfort and support, reflecting Your love and mercy to those in their care.

Lord, we trust in Your unfailing love and faithfulness, knowing that You are able to do immeasurably more than all we ask or imagine. We commit those who are sick into Your hands, confident that You are able to heal them according to Your will.

In Jesus' name we pray,
Amen.

Prayer for
Signs and Wonders

Heavenly Father,

We come before You with hearts full of awe and reverence, acknowledging Your sovereignty over all things, including signs and wonders. Your word tells us in **Acts 2:43** that many signs and wonders were done through the apostles, and we believe that You are the same yesterday, today, and forever.

Lord, we ask for Your miraculous intervention in our lives and in the world around us. Your word in **Mark 16:20** assures us that signs will accompany those who believe, and we humbly ask for Your signs and wonders to be manifest in our midst.

May Your power be displayed in healing the sick, restoring the brokenhearted, and setting the captives free. Your word in **Isaiah 35:5-6** promises that the eyes of the blind will be opened, the ears of the deaf unstopped, the lame will leap like a deer, and the tongue of the mute will shout for joy. We ask for these miracles to be realized in accordance with Your will.

Lord, we also pray for signs and wonders to accompany the preaching of Your Word, just as it did in the early church. Grant Your servants boldness and clarity as they proclaim the gospel, and confirm Your word with signs following, as You promised in **Mark 16:20**.

Father, we long to see Your glory revealed in mighty ways, not for our own glory, but for the advancement of Your kingdom and the proclamation of Your truth. May Your signs and wonders draw people to You, causing them to marvel at Your greatness and surrender their lives to You.

We thank You, Lord, for Your faithfulness and power to work miracles in our lives and in the world. May Your name be glorified through the signs and wonders that You perform, both now and forevermore.

In Jesus' name, we pray,
Amen.

Prayer for
Son

Heavenly Father,

I come before You with a heart full of gratitude for the precious gift of my son, *[Son's Name]*, whom You have graciously entrusted into my care. Your Word assures us in **Psalm 127:3, "Children are a heritage from the Lord, offspring a reward from him."** I thank You for the blessing he is to our family and for the joy and love he brings into our lives.

Lord, I lift up *[Son's Name]* to You, knowing that You have a perfect plan and purpose for his life. Your Word in **Jeremiah 29:11** reminds us, **"For I know the plans I have for you, declares the Lord, plans to prosper you and not to harm you, plans to give you hope and a future."** I pray that he may walk in the fullness of the destiny You have ordained for him.

Father, I ask for Your protection and guidance over *[Son's Name]*. Surround him with Your love and shield him from harm. Your Word in **Psalm 91:11** assures us, **"For he will command his angels concerning you to guard you in all your ways."** I pray that Your angels will watch over him and keep him safe wherever he goes.

Lord, I pray for *[Son's Name]*'s spiritual growth and relationship with You. May he come to know You personally and walk in Your ways all the days of his life. Your Word in **Proverbs 22:6** instructs us, **"Start children off on the way they should go, and even when they are old they will not turn from it."** I pray that he may grow in wisdom and stature, and in favor with You and with others.

Father, grant *[Son's Name]* good health, wisdom, and discernment in all his decisions. Help him to honor You in all that he does and to be a light shining brightly in this world. May he be a blessing to others and bring glory to Your name in everything he undertakes.

I commit *[Son's Name]* into Your loving hands, trusting in Your faithfulness and provision for his every need. May Your grace and peace be upon him now and always.

In Jesus' name, I pray,
Amen.

Prayer for
Spiritual Awareness

Heavenly Father,

We come before You with hearts open to Your leading and longing for deeper spiritual awareness. Your word teaches us in **Ephesians 1:17-18** that the God of our Lord Jesus Christ, the Father of glory, may give us the Spirit of wisdom and of revelation in the knowledge of Him, having the eyes of our hearts enlightened, that we may know what is the hope to which He has called us, what are the riches of His glorious inheritance in the saints.

Lord, we pray for spiritual discernment and understanding, that You would open the eyes of our hearts to see and comprehend the truths of Your Word and Your will for our lives. Your word in **Psalm 119:18** implores, **"Open my eyes that I may see wonderful things in your law."** Grant us spiritual insight and illumination, that we may walk in Your ways and grow in intimacy with You.

Father, we ask for a deeper awareness of Your presence in our lives. Help us to recognize Your voice speaking to us through Your Word, through prayer, and through the prompting of Your Holy Spirit. Your word assures us in **Isaiah 30:21, "Whether you turn to the right or to the left, your ears will hear a voice behind you, saying, "This is the way; walk in it."**

Lord, we pray for sensitivity to the Holy Spirit's leading and guidance. Your word in **John 16:13** promises, **"But when he, the Spirit of truth, comes, he will guide you into all the truth. He will not speak on his own; he will speak only what he hears, and he will tell you what is yet to come."** Help us to yield to the Holy Spirit's prompting, that we may walk in obedience and alignment with Your will.

Father, we ask for spiritual wisdom and maturity, that we may grow in Christ-likeness and bear fruit for Your kingdom. Lord, we thank You for the promise of Your presence and guidance in our lives. May we continually seek after You with all our hearts, knowing that You are the source of all wisdom, truth, and understanding.

In Jesus' name, we pray,
Amen.

Prayer for Spiritual Gifts

Heavenly Father,

We come before You with hearts open to Your leading and longing to discover and utilize the spiritual gifts You have graciously bestowed upon us. Your word teaches us in **1 Corinthians 12:4-7, "There are different kinds of gifts, but the same Spirit distributes them. There are different kinds of service, but the same Lord. There are different kinds of working, but in all of them and in everyone it is the same God at work. Now to each one the manifestation of the Spirit is given for the common good."** Lord, we acknowledge that You have uniquely equipped each of us with spiritual gifts for the edification of the body of Christ and for the advancement of Your kingdom. We pray for wisdom and discernment to recognize and develop the spiritual gifts You have entrusted to us.

Father, Your word instructs us in **1 Peter 4:10-11, "Each of you should use whatever gift you have received to serve others, as faithful stewards of God's grace in its various forms. If anyone speaks, they should do so as one who speaks the very words of God. If anyone serves, they should do so with the strength God provides, so that in all things God may be praised through Jesus Christ. To him be the glory and the power for ever and ever. Amen."**

Lord, we ask that You would reveal to us the specific spiritual gifts You have given us, whether it be the gift of prophecy, evangelism, apostleship, serving, teaching, encouraging, giving, leadership, mercy, or any other gift. Grant us the courage and humility to step out in faith and use these gifts for the building up of the body of Christ and for Your glory. Father, we pray for unity within the body of Christ, recognizing and honoring the diverse spiritual gifts You have distributed among us. Help us to value and appreciate one another's gifts, working together in harmony and mutual respect for the common good.

Lord, empower us by Your Spirit to exercise our spiritual gifts with boldness, compassion, and love. Your word assures us in **2 Timothy 1:7, "For the Spirit God gave us does not make us timid, but gives us power, love and self-discipline."** May we walk in the fullness of Your Spirit, using our gifts to impact lives, transform communities, and bring glory to Your name.

Father, we surrender ourselves afresh to You, inviting You to work through us for Your purposes. May our lives be a testimony to Your grace and power as we steward the spiritual gifts You have entrusted to us.

In Jesus' name, we pray,
Amen.

Prayer for
Spiritual Warfare

Heavenly Father,

I come before You today aware of the spiritual battles that surround me. Your Word in **Ephesians 6:12** reminds me that our struggle is not against flesh and blood, but against the rulers, against the authorities, against the powers of this dark world and against the spiritual forces of evil in the heavenly realms. Therefore, I put on the full armor of God, so that I can take my stand against the devil's schemes.

Sanctify me Lord by the truth, as Your Word is truth, as it is written in **John 17:17**. Help me to walk in truth and integrity, and to discern the lies and deceptions of the enemy.

As per **Ephesians 6:14**, I put on the breastplate of righteousness, which guards my heart against the accusations and attacks of the enemy. Cover me with Your righteousness, Lord, and help me to live a life that is pleasing to You.

I shod my feet with the readiness that comes from the gospel of peace according to **Ephesians 6:15**. Lead me in the paths of peace, Lord, and help me to share the message of Your love and salvation with others. I take up the shield of faith, with which I can extinguish all the flaming arrows of the evil one as stated in **Ephesians 6:16**. Strengthen my faith, Lord, and help me to trust in Your promises even in the midst of trials and tribulations.

I put on the helmet of salvation, knowing that I am redeemed and saved by the blood of Jesus Christ as promised in **Ephesians 6:17**. Guard my mind, Lord, and protect me from doubt, fear, and despair.

As I was taught in **Ephesians 6:17**, I take up the sword of the Spirit, which is the Word of God. Help me to wield Your Word effectively, Lord, and to use it to combat the lies and temptations of the enemy. Finally, I pray in the Spirit on all occasions as written in **Ephesians 6:18** with all kinds of prayers and requests. Fill me with Your Holy Spirit, Lord, and help me to pray without ceasing, seeking Your guidance and strength in every situation.

Thank You, Lord, for the victory that is mine in Christ Jesus. Help me to stand firm in the faith, knowing that You are with me always.

In Jesus' name, I pray,
Amen.

Prayer for Strength to Forgive Others

Heavenly Father,

I come before You in need of Your strength and guidance to forgive those who have wronged me, as Your Word instructs us. In **Ephesians 4:32**, You told us, **"Be kind and compassionate to one another, forgiving each other, just as in Christ God forgave you."** Lord, I ask for the grace to extend the same forgiveness to others that You have shown to me.

Forgiving others can be challenging, but I know that with You, all things are possible. Your Word in **Philippians 4:13** assures us, **"I can do all this through him who gives me strength."** Give me the strength, Lord, to release any bitterness, resentment, or anger I may be harboring in my heart. Help me to let go of the pain and hurt inflicted upon me, knowing that forgiveness is not condoning the wrongdoing but releasing myself from its hold.

Just as You have forgiven me of my sins, help me to forgive others from my heart. Your Word in **Colossians 3:13** urges us, **"Bear with each other and forgive one another if any of you has a grievance against someone. Forgive as the Lord forgave you."** May I reflect Your love and mercy by extending forgiveness freely, as You have freely forgiven me.

Lord, I surrender my hurt and pain to You, knowing that You are the healer of all wounds. Your Word in **Psalm 147:3** reminds us, **"He heals the brokenhearted and binds up their wounds."** Heal my wounded heart, Lord, and fill it with Your peace and love. Help me to release the burden of unforgiveness and to walk in the freedom of forgiveness.

I pray for those who have wronged me, Lord. Bless them, and may they come to know Your love and forgiveness in their own lives. Help me to see them through Your eyes, with compassion and understanding, and to pray for their well-being.

Thank You, Lord, for Your grace that empowers me to forgive. May Your Spirit continue to work in me, transforming my heart and mind to reflect Your love and forgiveness more fully each day.

In Jesus' name, I pray,
Amen.

Prayer for
Strength

Heavenly Father,

We come before You today, acknowledging our need for Your strength in our lives. Your Word reminds us in **Isaiah 40:29, "He gives strength to the weary and increases the power of the weak."** Lord, we lean on You for the strength that we lack.

Grant us, O Lord, strength to face the challenges and trials of life. When we feel weary and burdened, may we find our strength in You, knowing that You are our refuge and our fortress.

We pray for physical strength, Lord. Strengthen our bodies, energize our minds, and renew our spirits. Help us to care for our bodies as temples of Your Holy Spirit, so that we may serve You faithfully.

Grant us emotional strength, Lord. Comfort us in times of sorrow, heal us in times of brokenness, and fill us with Your peace that surpasses all understanding. May we find our strength in Your presence, knowing that You are always with us.

We pray for spiritual strength, Lord. Help us to stand firm in our faith, even when the world around us may shake. Equip us with the armor of God, as mentioned in **Ephesians 6:10-11, "Finally, be strong in the Lord and in his mighty power. Put on the full armor of God, so that you can take your stand against the devil's schemes."** May we be strong in the Lord and in the power of his might.

Lord, we ask for strength to fulfill the purposes You have for our lives. Give us courage to step out in faith, boldness to proclaim Your truth, and perseverance to endure until the end.

In Jesus' name we pray,
Amen.

Prayer for Submission

Heavenly Father,

I come before You with a humble heart, acknowledging Your sovereignty and lordship over my life. Your Word in **James 4:7** teaches us to submit ourselves to You, for You are the ultimate authority. I surrender my will and desires to You, trusting in Your wisdom and perfect plan for my life.

Lord, forgive me for the times when I have sought to control my own path and ignored Your guidance. Help me to let go of my own ambitions and selfish desires, and to embrace Your will for me with obedience and humility as written in **Proverbs 3:5-6**.

Father, teach me to trust in Your goodness and faithfulness, even when I cannot see the outcome. Give me a submissive heart that is willing to follow wherever You lead, knowing that Your plans are always for my welfare and not for harm as I was taught in **Jeremiah 29:11**.

Lord, I pray for the grace to submit to the authorities You have placed over me, whether it be in the government, the church, or the workplace as instructed in **Romans 13:1**. Help me to honor those in positions of authority and to submit to their leadership with respect and humility.

Father, I surrender every aspect of my life to You, the big decisions and the small ones, the joys and the struggles, the victories and the defeats. May Your will be done in me and through me, for Your glory and the advancement of Your kingdom as written in **Matthew 6:10**.

Lord, I thank You for the example of Jesus, who submitted himself fully to Your will, even unto death on the cross as mentioned in **Philippians 2:8**. Help me to follow his example of obedience and submission, trusting in Your plan and resting in Your love.

In Jesus' name, I pray,
Amen.

Prayer for Success

Heavenly Father,

We come before You today with hearts full of gratitude for Your abundant blessings and the opportunities You have given us. Your Word in **Joshua 1:8** teaches us, **"Keep this Book of the Law always on your lips; meditate on it day and night, so that you may be careful to do everything written in it. Then you will be prosperous and successful."** We seek Your guidance and wisdom as we strive for success in our endeavors.

Lord, we commit our plans and goals into Your hands, trusting in Your providence and sovereignty. Your Word in **Proverbs 16:3** assures us, **"Commit to the Lord whatever you do, and he will establish your plans."** May our efforts align with Your will, and may You establish our steps toward success.

Grant us, O Lord, the diligence, perseverance, and integrity to pursue our goals with excellence. Help us to work as unto You, knowing that our labor in the Lord is not in vain as written in **1 Corinthians 15:58**. May we glorify You in all that we do, whether in word or deed.

Father, we pray for discernment to recognize the opportunities You place before us and the courage to seize them. Your Word in **Jeremiah 29:11** reminds us, **"For I know the plans I have for you, plans to prosper you and not to harm you, plans to give you hope and a future."** May we trust in Your plans for our success, knowing that You have our best interests at heart.

Lord, we also ask for Your favor to be upon us as we strive for success. Your Word in **Psalm 90:17** petitions, **"May the favor of the Lord our God rest on us; establish the work of our hands for us—yes, establish the work of our hands."** May Your favor open doors of opportunity and bring success to our endeavors.

We surrender our desires for success into Your hands, knowing that You are able to do immeasurably more than all we ask or imagine, according to Your power that is at work within us as promised in **Ephesians 3:20**. May our success bring glory to Your name and further the work of Your kingdom on earth.

In Jesus' name we pray,
Amen.

Prayer for
Teachers

Heavenly Father,

We come before You with hearts full of gratitude for the teachers You have placed in our lives. Your word tells us in **James 3:1, "Not many of you should become teachers, my fellow believers, because you know that we who teach will be judged more strictly."** We thank You, Lord, for the dedication, wisdom, and guidance that our teachers provide each day.

Father, we pray for our teachers, both past and present. We ask for Your blessing upon them as they fulfill the important role of shaping and molding young minds. May they be filled with Your wisdom and discernment as they impart knowledge and understanding to their students.

Grant our teachers patience, compassion, and grace as they interact with their students. Help them to see each student as a unique individual created in Your image, deserving of love, respect, and encouragement. May they inspire their students to reach their full potential and pursue excellence in all areas of life.

Father, we lift up our teachers' needs and concerns to You. Provide them with the strength and energy they need to meet the demands of their profession. Protect them from burnout and exhaustion and give them a sense of fulfillment and purpose in their work.

We pray for unity and harmony among the faculty and staff of our schools. May they work together as a team, supporting and encouraging one another in their shared mission of educating and nurturing young hearts and minds.

Lord, we ask for Your guidance and wisdom for our teachers as they navigate the challenges of the classroom. Help them to find creative solutions to problems and give them the courage to face difficult situations with grace and integrity.

We thank You, Lord, for the impact our teachers have on our lives and on future generations. May they continue to inspire, encourage, and empower their students to become lifelong learners and followers of Your truth.

In Jesus' name, we pray,
Amen.

Prayer for Temptations

Heavenly Father,

We come before You humbly, acknowledging our weaknesses and vulnerabilities to temptation. Your word teaches us in **1 Corinthians 10:13** that no temptation has overtaken us except what is common to mankind. And You are faithful; You will not let us be tempted beyond what we can bear. But when we are tempted, You will also provide a way out so that we can endure it.

Lord, we ask for Your strength and guidance in the face of temptation. Help us to recognize the schemes of the enemy and to stand firm in Your truth. Your word in **James 4:7** tells us to submit ourselves to You, resist the devil, and he will flee from us. Give us the wisdom to resist temptation and to flee from the desires of the flesh that wage war against our souls as instructed in **1 Peter 2:11**.

Father, we pray for discernment to recognize the lies and deceptions of the enemy. Your word in **Ephesians 6:11** instructs us to put on the full armor of God so that we can stand against the schemes of the devil. Help us to be vigilant and alert, taking up the shield of faith, the helmet of salvation, the sword of the Spirit, which is Your word, and the belt of truth to withstand the attacks of the evil one.

Lord, we ask for Your Holy Spirit to empower us to overcome temptation. Your word in **Galatians 5:16** encourages us to walk by the Spirit and not gratify the desires of the flesh. Fill us afresh with Your Spirit, that we may bear the fruit of love, joy, peace, patience, kindness, goodness, faithfulness, gentleness, and self-control according to **Galatians 5:22-23.**

Father, we pray for accountability and support from our brothers and sisters in Christ. Your word in **Hebrews 10:24-25** instructs us to consider how we spur one another on toward love and good deeds, not giving up meeting together, as some are in the habit of doing, but encouraging one another.

Lord, we thank You for Your promise to help us in times of temptation. May we always look to You for strength and find refuge in Your presence. As written in **Hebrews 12:2**, help us to keep our eyes fixed on Jesus, the author and perfecter of our faith, who endured the cross for us.

In Jesus' name, we pray,
Amen.

Prayer for Thanksgiving

Heavenly Father,

I come before You with a heart brimming with gratitude and thanksgiving for all that You have done in my life. Your faithfulness and goodness have been evident in every season, and I am overwhelmed by Your love and provision.

Lord, I thank You for Your unwavering presence in my life. You have promised in **Deuteronomy 31:6**, never to leave me nor forsake me, and Your faithfulness endures forever. Thank You for walking with me through every trial and triumph, and for being my constant source of strength and comfort.

I thank You, Lord, for Your boundless love and grace. You loved me even when I was lost in sin as written in **Ephesians 2:4-5**, and You sent Your Son, Jesus Christ, to redeem me and reconcile me to Yourself as promised in **John 3:16**. Thank You for the sacrificial death of Jesus on the cross, which paid the price for my sins and brought me into a right relationship with You. Lord, I thank You for the countless blessings You have bestowed upon me. You have provided for all my needs according to Your riches in glory as mentioned n **Philippians 4:19**, and Your mercies are new every morning as promised in **Lamentations 3:22-23**. Thank You for Your provision, protection, and guidance, and for the abundance of Your grace in my life.

I thank You, Lord, for the gift of salvation and eternal life. Through faith in Jesus Christ, I have been adopted into Your family as Your beloved child as reflected in **Ephesians 1:5**, and I have the hope of spending eternity with You in heaven as promised in **John 14:2-3**. Thank You for the assurance of salvation and for the promise of everlasting life in Your presence.

Lord, I thank You for the work You are doing in my life and in the lives of those around me. You are constantly at work, shaping and molding us into the image of Christ according to **Romans 8:28-29**, and You have a purpose and plan for each of us as promised in **Jeremiah 29:11**.

Thank You for Your faithfulness in completing the good work You have begun in us. I praise You, Lord, with all my heart, soul, mind, and strength. May my life be a living testimony of Your goodness and grace, and may I never cease to give You thanks and praise for all that You have done and continue to do in my life.

In Jesus' name, I pray,
Amen.

Prayer for
The Persecuted

Heavenly Father,

We lift up to You today all those who are persecuted for their faith around the world. Your word reminds us in **Matthew 5:10-12, "Blessed are those who are persecuted because of righteousness, for theirs is the kingdom of heaven. Blessed are you when people insult you, persecute you and falsely say all kinds of evil against you because of me. Rejoice and be glad, because great is your reward in heaven, for in the same way they persecuted the prophets who were before you."**

Lord, we pray for our brothers and sisters who are facing persecution because of their unwavering commitment to following You. Strengthen them with Your Spirit, Lord, and fill them with courage, hope, and endurance in the midst of their trials.

Protect them from harm, O Lord, and shield them from the schemes of the enemy. Provide them with supernatural peace that surpasses all understanding, knowing that You are with them always, even in the darkest of times.

Father, we ask for justice and righteousness to prevail in the face of persecution. May those who persecute Your people come to know the truth of Your gospel and experience Your transforming love and grace.

Give wisdom and discernment to those in authority, Lord, that they may uphold justice and protect the rights and freedoms of all people, including those who are persecuted for their faith. Lord, we pray for unity among believers around the world, that we may stand in solidarity with our persecuted brothers and sisters, offering them support, encouragement, and fervent prayer.

May Your word be a source of strength and comfort to those who are persecuted, reminding them of Your promise in **Isaiah 41:10, "So do not fear, for I am with you; do not be dismayed, for I am your God. I will strengthen you and help you; I will uphold you with my righteous right hand."**

We thank You, Lord, for the faithfulness and perseverance of Your persecuted church. May their witness shine brightly in the darkness, drawing many to faith in Christ and bringing glory to Your name.

In Jesus' name, we pray,
Amen.

Prayer for Unity

Heavenly Father,

We come before You today as Your children, united in faith and love, seeking Your guidance and blessing. Your Word teaches us the importance of unity among believers, and we desire to experience the fullness of that unity in our lives and in our communities.

Lord, You have called us to be one body, with Christ as our head as urged in **1 Corinthians 12:12-13**. Help us to live in harmony with one another, bearing with one another in love and striving to maintain the unity of the Spirit in the bond of peace as instructed in **Ephesians 4:2-3**.

Father, we confess that there are times when we allow division, discord, and strife to come between us. Forgive us for our failures to love one another as You have loved us and taught us in **John 13:34-35**. Give us hearts that are humble and tender, willing to forgive one another and to seek reconciliation when conflicts arise as written in **Colossians 3:13-14**.

Lord Jesus, You prayed for unity among Your disciples, that they may be one, just as You and the Father are one as we learn in **John 17:20-23**. May the same spirit of unity that dwells in You also dwell in us, so that the world may know that You have sent us and that You love us as You have loved Yourself.

Holy Spirit, we invite You to come and fill us afresh with Your presence and power. Bind us together in perfect unity, enabling us to serve one another in love and to bear witness to the world of Your transforming grace as shown in **Galatians 5:22-23**.

Lord, we thank You for the gift of unity that You offer us through Your Son, Jesus Christ. Help us to cherish and protect this precious gift, knowing that it is only through our unity that we can truly reflect Your love and bring glory to Your name.

In Jesus' name, we pray,
Amen.

Prayer for Victims of Disaster

Heavenly Father,

We come before You with heavy hearts, grieving for those who have been affected by disasters around the world. Your Word assures us in **Psalm 34:18** that You are near to the brokenhearted and save the crushed in spirit. We lift up to You all the victims of disasters, whether they be natural calamities, accidents, or tragedies caused by human actions.

Lord, we pray for Your comfort to be upon those who are mourning the loss of loved ones. Your Word reminds us in **2 Corinthians 1:3-4, "Praise be to the God and Father of our Lord Jesus Christ, the Father of compassion and the God of all comfort, who comforts us in all our troubles, so that we can comfort those in any trouble with the comfort we ourselves receive from God."** May they find solace in Your loving embrace and experience the peace that surpasses all understanding.

Father, we ask for Your provision and protection for those who have been displaced from their homes or are facing uncertain futures. Your Word assures us in **Psalm 91:1-2, "Whoever dwells in the shelter of the Most High will rest in the shadow of the Almighty. I will say of the Lord, "He is my refuge and my fortress, my God, in whom I trust.""** Shelter them under the shadow of Your wings and provide for their every need according to Your riches in glory.

Lord Jesus, we pray for Your healing touch upon those who have been injured or traumatized by the devastation they have experienced. Your Word declares in **Psalm 147:3, "He heals the brokenhearted and binds up their wounds."** Bring physical, emotional, and spiritual restoration to their lives, and may they find hope and strength in You. Father, we intercede for the communities and nations affected by disasters, praying for unity, resilience, and perseverance in the face of adversity. Your Word encourages us in **Romans 12:12 to "Be joyful in hope, patient in affliction, faithful in prayer."** May they find hope in You, patience in their trials, and strength to rebuild and recover.

Lord, we ask for Your wisdom and guidance for all those involved in relief efforts, including first responders, aid workers, and volunteers. Your Word instructs us in **Proverbs 3:5-6, "Trust in the Lord with all your heart and lean not on your own understanding; in all your ways submit to him, and he will make your paths straight."** Guide their steps, grant them discernment, and empower them to be Your hands and feet of love and compassion.

Father, we commit all the victims of disasters into Your loving hands, trusting in Your unfailing love and faithfulness to bring beauty from ashes. May Your name be glorified as You work through the brokenness of this world to bring about redemption and restoration.

In Jesus' name, we pray,
Amen.

Prayer for Victory

Heavenly Father,

I come before You today with a heart full of gratitude for the victory that is already mine through Jesus Christ, my Lord and Savior. Your Word declares in **2 Corinthians 2:14**, that You always lead us in triumph in Christ, and I thank You for the assurance of victory that I have in Him.

Lord, I pray that You would strengthen me with Your mighty power, filling me with courage and confidence to face every challenge and obstacle that comes my way. Your Word assures me in **1 John 4:4**, that greater is He who is in me than he who is in the world, and I take hold of that truth as I stand firm in faith.

I declare victory over every trial, temptation, and adversity that I may encounter, knowing that I am more than a conqueror through Him who loved me as written in **Romans 8:37**. I am persuaded that neither death nor life, neither angels nor demons, neither the present nor the future, nor any powers, neither height nor depth, nor anything else in all creation, will be able to separate me from the love of God that is in Christ Jesus our Lord as promised in **Romans 8:38-39**.

Father, I thank You for the weapons of warfare that You have provided for me, which are mighty through God for pulling down strongholds according to **2 Corinthians 10:4**.

As mentioned in **Ephesians 6:11**, I put on the full armor of God so that I may be able to stand firm against the schemes of the devil, and I take up the shield of faith, the helmet of salvation, and the sword of the Spirit, which is the Word of God as stated in **Ephesians 6:16-17**.

I praise You, Lord, for the victory that is mine in Christ Jesus. Help me to walk in faith and obedience, knowing that You are always with me, fighting on my behalf. May my life be a testament to Your faithfulness and the power of Your love.

In Jesus' name, I pray,
Amen.

Prayer for Wife

Heavenly Father,

I come before You today with a heart full of gratitude for the precious gift of my wife. Your word tells us in **Proverbs 18:22, "He who finds a wife finds what is good and receives favor from the Lord."** Thank You for blessing me with her presence in my life.

Lord, I lift up my wife to You, knowing that she is fearfully and wonderfully made in Your image. I thank You for her love, her strength, and her unwavering support. Your word reminds us in **Ephesians 5:25, "Husbands, love your wives, just as Christ loved the church and gave himself up for her."** Help me to love my wife sacrificially, just as Christ loves the church.

Father, I pray for my wife's health and well-being. Grant her physical strength, emotional peace, and spiritual vitality. Your word assures us in **Psalm 103:2-3, "Praise the Lord, my soul, and forget not all his benefits—who forgives all your sins and heals all your diseases."** May Your healing touch be upon her, restoring her to fullness of health.

Lord, I pray for my wife's spiritual journey. Draw her closer to You each day, deepening her faith and trust in Your goodness and mercy. Your word tells us in **Psalm 23:3, "He refreshes my soul. He guides me along the right paths for his name's sake."** Guide her in the paths of righteousness, and may she find refreshment and renewal in Your presence.

Father, I ask for Your protection over my wife, both physically and spiritually. Guard her against harm and keep her safe from the attacks of the enemy. Your word assures us in **Psalm 91:11-12, "For he will command his angels concerning you to guard you in all your ways; they will lift you up in their hands, so that you will not strike your foot against a stone."** Surround her with Your angels and cover her with Your peace.

Lord, I thank You for the blessing my wife is in my life and in the lives of others. Help me to cherish her, honor her, and support her in all things. Your word reminds us in **Proverbs 31:10, "A wife of noble character who can find? She is worth far more than rubies."** May I always recognize and appreciate the incredible gift that she is. I commit my wife into Your loving hands, trusting in Your faithfulness to watch over her and to guide her in all her ways.

In Jesus' name I pray,
Amen.

Prayer for Wildlife and Animals

Heavenly Father,

We come before You with gratitude for the beauty and diversity of Your creation, including the wildlife and animals that inhabit the earth. Your Word declares in **Psalm 104:24, "How many are your works, Lord! In wisdom you made them all; the earth is full of your creatures."** Thank You for entrusting us with stewardship over these precious beings.

Lord, we lift up to You all the wildlife and animals across the globe. You have declared in **Genesis 1:25, "God made the wild animals according to their kinds, the livestock according to their kinds, and all the creatures that move along the ground according to their kinds. And God saw that it was good."** We pray for their protection, preservation, and well-being.

Father, we acknowledge that humanity's actions have often led to harm and exploitation of wildlife and animals. Your Word teaches us in **Proverbs 12:10, "The righteous care for the needs of their animals, but the kindest acts of the wicked are cruel."** Forgive us for our neglect and mistreatment and grant us hearts of compassion and responsibility toward all living creatures. Lord Jesus, we pray for conservation efforts and initiatives aimed at preserving habitats and species. Your Word affirms in **Psalm 50:10-11, "for every animal of the forest is mine, and the cattle on a thousand hills. I know every bird in the mountains, and the insects in the fields are mine."** May we be good stewards of Your creation, working to protect and restore the balance of nature.

Father, we ask for Your wisdom and guidance in addressing issues such as poaching, habitat destruction, and climate change that threaten the survival of wildlife and animals. Your Word promises in **Job 12:7-10, "But ask the animals, and they will teach you, or the birds in the sky, and they will tell you; or speak to the earth, and it will teach you, or let the fish in the sea inform you. Which of all these does not know that the hand of the Lord has done this? In his hand is the life of every creature and the breath of all mankind."**

Lord, may we be mindful of our interconnectedness with all creation and act with love, compassion, and responsibility toward every living creature. Help us to be voices for the voiceless and advocates for the protection of wildlife and animals. We commit the care of wildlife and animals into Your hands, trusting in Your sovereignty and compassion. Your Word assures us in **Matthew 10:29, "Are not two sparrows sold for a penny? Yet not one of them will fall to the ground outside your Father's care."** Thank You, Lord, for Your unfailing love and provision.

In Jesus' name, we pray,
Amen.

Prayer for
Wisdom

Heavenly Father,

We humbly come before You, recognizing our need for Your wisdom and guidance in every aspect of our lives. Your word tells us in **James 1:5, "If any of you lacks wisdom, you should ask God, who gives generously to all without finding fault, and it will be given to you."** Lord, we ask for wisdom today, knowing that You are the source of all wisdom and understanding.

Grant us, O Lord, wisdom to discern Your will in every decision we make. Help us to seek Your guidance in all things, trusting in Your perfect plan for our lives.

We pray for wisdom in our relationships, Lord. Help us to love others with Your love, to forgive as You have forgiven us, and to be peacemakers in a world filled with conflict and division.

Grant us wisdom in our work and studies, Lord. Help us to excel in our endeavors, using our talents and abilities for Your glory and the benefit of others.

Lord, we ask for wisdom in handling our finances. Help us to be good stewards of the resources You have entrusted to us, using them wisely and generously for Your kingdom purposes.

We pray for wisdom in times of uncertainty and trial. Your word assures us in **Proverbs 3:5-6, "Trust in the Lord with all your heart and lean not on your own understanding; in all your ways submit to him, and he will make your paths straight."** May we trust in You completely, knowing that You will guide us through every difficulty.

Fill us, O Lord, with Your Holy Spirit, who is the spirit of wisdom and revelation. Open the eyes of our hearts to know You more deeply and to understand Your will for our lives.

In Jesus' name we pray,
Amen.

Prayer for
Workplace

Heavenly Father,

We come before You today with hearts full of gratitude for the opportunity to work and serve in our respective workplaces. Thank You for the skills and talents You have entrusted to us, and for the opportunities to make a difference in the lives of others through our work.

As it is written in **Colossians 3:23-24, "Whatever you do, work at it with all your heart, as working for the Lord, not for human masters, since you know that you will receive an inheritance from the Lord as a reward. It is the Lord Christ you are serving."**

Lord, we lift up our workplaces to You. We pray for Your presence to be felt in every office, cubicle, factory floor, and storefront. May Your peace, wisdom, and grace penetrate every interaction and decision made within our workplace. As it is written in **Proverbs 3:5-6, "Trust in the Lord with all your heart and lean not on your own understanding; in all your ways submit to him, and he will make your paths straight."**

Grant us, O Lord, the strength and perseverance to carry out our duties with excellence and integrity. Help us to work diligently, as unto You, and to treat our colleagues and customers with kindness, respect, and compassion. As it is written in **Ephesians 4:32, "Be kind and compassionate to one another, forgiving each other, just as in Christ God forgave you."**

We pray for unity among our coworkers, that we may work together harmoniously towards common goals. Help us to support and encourage one another, to celebrate each other's successes, and to bear one another's burdens. As it is written in **Romans 12:10, "Be devoted to one another in love. Honor one another above yourselves."**

Lord, we also lift up our supervisors, managers, and leaders. Grant them wisdom and discernment as they make decisions that impact the lives of their employees. Help them to lead with humility, fairness, and compassion, seeking the well-being of all who work under their authority.

As it is written in **Proverbs 11:14, "For lack of guidance a nation falls, but victory is won through many advisers."** Guard our hearts and minds from negativity, gossip, and discord in the workplace. Instead, fill us with gratitude, joy, and a spirit of cooperation as we strive to fulfill our responsibilities.

Prayer for Workplace

As it is written in **Philippians 4:8, "Finally, brothers and sisters, whatever is true, whatever is noble, whatever is right, whatever is pure, whatever is lovely, whatever is admirable—if anything is excellent or praiseworthy—think about such things."**

May our work bring honor and glory to Your name, Lord, as we strive to be salt and light in the world. Use us as instruments of Your love and grace, shining brightly in our workplaces and making a positive impact on those around us. As it is written in **Matthew 5:16, "In the same way, let your light shine before others, that they may see your good deeds and glorify your Father in heaven."**

In Jesus' name we pray,
Amen.

Prayer for Worship Choir and Music Team

Heavenly Father,

We gather before you today as a worship choir and music team, grateful for the privilege and responsibility to lead your people in praise and adoration. We recognize the power of music to touch hearts and draw souls closer to you, and we humbly offer our talents and gifts to glorify your name.

As we come together to lift our voices and instruments in worship, we pray for your anointing and presence to fill this place. May your Holy Spirit guide our rehearsals and performances, that every note sung and played may resonate with the beauty of your holiness.

Lord, you have gifted each member of this choir and music team with unique abilities and talents. Help us to use these gifts wisely and faithfully, to serve you and minister to others. Teach us to harmonize with one another in spirit and in truth, that our music may be a pleasing offering to you.

In the book of **Psalm 96:1-2**, David declares: **"Sing to the Lord a new song; sing to the Lord, all the earth. Sing to the Lord, praise his name; proclaim his salvation day after day"**. May we heed David's call and sing with joy and thanksgiving, declaring your salvation and proclaiming your praises to all the earth.

Lord, we also pray for unity and humility among our team members. Help us to put aside personal preferences and agendas, and to work together in love and harmony. May our unity be a testimony to your love and grace, drawing others into deeper relationship with you.

Finally, we lift up our worship leaders and directors, that you would grant them wisdom, discernment, and vision as they lead us. May they be filled with your Spirit and guided by your word in all their decisions and direction.

We commit ourselves and our music into your hands, Lord, trusting that you will use it for your glory and the advancement of your kingdom. May our songs of worship rise as a sweet fragrance before your throne, bringing honor and glory to your holy name.

In Jesus' name we pray,
Amen.

Prayer for
World Peace

Heavenly Father,

We come before You with heavy hearts, longing for peace to prevail in our troubled world. Your word tells us in **John 14:27, "Peace I leave with you; my peace I give you. I do not give to you as the world gives. Do not let your hearts be troubled and do not be afraid."** We lift up our prayers for peace, knowing that You are the ultimate source of true peace.

Lord, we pray for an end to violence, conflict, and war in every corner of the globe. Your word in **Psalm 46:9** declares that You make wars cease to the ends of the earth. We ask for Your intervention to bring about reconciliation, understanding, and forgiveness among nations and peoples.

Father, we lift up those who are suffering due to conflict and oppression. Comfort them in their distress and provide them with the strength and courage to endure. Help us to be agents of peace and compassion, reaching out to those in need and working tirelessly for justice and reconciliation.

We pray for world leaders, as Your word instructs us in **1 Timothy 2:1-2**, to pray for all those in authority, that we may live peaceful and quiet lives in all godliness and holiness. Grant them wisdom, discernment, and humility as they navigate complex geopolitical issues and seek solutions to long-standing conflicts.

Lord, we ask for a spirit of unity among nations, that we may set aside our differences and work together for the common good. Your word in **Ephesians 4:3** urges us to make every effort to keep the unity of the Spirit through the bond of peace. May Your Spirit move in the hearts of leaders and citizens alike, drawing us closer to one another in love and understanding.

Father, we pray for the protection of those who serve in the military and humanitarian organizations, risking their lives to promote peace and alleviate suffering. Strengthen them in their noble endeavors and guide their efforts towards lasting peace and stability.

Finally, Lord, we pray for the ultimate fulfillment of Your promise of peace, when Your kingdom will reign in its fullness, and swords will be turned into plowshares as stated in **Isaiah 2:4**. Until that glorious day, help us to be peacemakers in our communities, shining Your light and sharing Your love wherever we go.

In Jesus' name, we pray,
Amen.

Thank you

Dear Reader,

As we come to the end of this collection of prayers, we want to express our heartfelt gratitude to you. Thank you for journeying with us through these pages, seeking solace, guidance, and connection with God. It has been our honor and privilege to accompany you in prayer.

Each prayer in this book is a heartfelt expression of faith, drawing inspiration from the Word of God and the rich tapestry of Christian tradition. But prayer is not merely about reciting words written by others; it is about engaging in a personal, intimate conversation with God.

We encourage you to make these prayers your own. Feel free to adapt them, personalize them, and make them resonate with your unique voice and experiences. The Bible assures us in **Romans 8:26-27** that **"the Spirit helps us in our weakness. For we do not know what to pray for as we ought, but the Spirit himself intercedes for us with groanings too deep for words."** Trust that the Holy Spirit will guide you as you pray.

Remember, prayer is not a one-way conversation but a dialogue with God Almighty. Take time to listen to God's voice, to be still in His presence, and to discern His will for your life. Let these prayers serve as a springboard for your own spiritual journey, leading you deeper into relationship with God.

May you find comfort, strength, and hope in the presence of the Almighty. May your prayer life be a source of joy, peace, and transformation. And may you walk confidently in the knowledge that God hears your prayers and delights in communing with you.

Wishing you amazing Divine Conversations with the one and only, Almighty God, in the name of His Precious Son, Jesus Christ, and with the guidance of the Holy Spirit.

With deepest gratitude and blessings,

Norman J. Sinappen

About The Author

Norman J. Sinappen was born in the bustling city of Kuala Lumpur in 1980, into the loving embrace of his parents, Sinappen and Margaret. Growing up alongside his three younger siblings, Carolyn Jesurina, Helena Jesurose, and Jeremiah Jesuran, Norman was immersed in a family environment rich with love, faith, and spiritual nourishment.

At the tender age of 15, Norman experienced a profound transformation when he encountered the life-changing message of Jesus Christ, leading him to embrace a life of faith as a born-again Christian. Since then, his journey has been marked by a series of divine interventions and miraculous encounters that have shaped his faith and strengthened his conviction in God's unfailing love and grace.

Drawing inspiration from his personal experiences and deep-rooted faith, Norman has authored two prior books: "The Best Quotes from the Bible" and "BELiEVE," which reflect his passion for sharing the timeless truths found within the pages of Scripture.

As the founder of The HighGround Ministries, Norman seeks to impart his insights on various aspects of faith, life, and spirituality, grounded in the teachings of the Bible. He views himself as a perpetual student of God's Word, constantly seeking to deepen his understanding and share the gospel message with others around the globe.

In addition to his literary pursuits, Norman is embarking on a transformative journey as a first-year student at a Bible College, pursuing a Master of Divinity degree to further equip himself for ministry and service.

Norman resides in the picturesque city of Geneva, Switzerland, where he, together with his beloved wife Shirley and their cherished daughter Audrey Aryn, find joy in serving the Lord and spreading His message of love and redemption.

Connect with Norman on social media:
YOUTUBE: https://www.Youtube.com/@normansinappenhm
X: https://www.twitter.com/normanministry
FACEBOOK: https://www.tinyurl.com/NormanJSinappen
INSTAGRAM: https://www.instagram.com/highground_ministries
TIKTOK: https://www.tiktok.com/@norman.j.sinappen

Notes

Notes

Notes